Taking Charge
Life and in Business Life

John H. Olsen

Taking Charge Life and in Business Life
Copyright © 2024 by John H. Olsen

ISBN
978-1-962868-38-9 (Paperback)
978-1-962868-39-6 (eBook)
978-1-962868-60-0 (Hardcover)

TAKING CHARGE
LIFE AND IN BUSINESS LIFE

Olsen

To my dad and mom-Albert Olsen Jr. & Viola D. Olsen

TABLE OF CONTENTS

INTRODUCTION

~ § ~

The cover of this book is made of two parts. The Norse rune stones spell out our surname Olsen.

The Norse meaning of each stone is O – Property, Homeland, Inheritance L – Water, Lake S – Sun, Salvation E – Horse, Friendship N – Need, Necessity. The fire and forge represent something I discovered during my research of the Olsen's. I discovered Great-Great Grand-Pa Olsen was a Journeymen blacksmith in Norway. My Great Grand-Pa brought the Olsen surname to United States via Denmark on the 9th of July 1870 landing in New York. The Mormon Church helped them to come to the United States from Norway. They traveled on to Washington Island, WI and then settling in Provo, Utah. A surname that has been carried on by two generations before me and now my sons Lars and James.

We were a melted family that was made of lots of Half-brothers and Half-sisters from their previous marriages. That part of my family was ripped away from their mother by a vindictive ex-husband. I was only but a baby when this had happened so really I never knew what was going on at that time. I knew of them, but those are only vague memories.

Yes, I can say I was robbed of knowing my brothers and sister better, but the real victims were my parents, brothers and sister. A person may have a pleasant smile on their face hiding the pain and lose in their heart. A face may never tell the whole story of their life. Can you really tell what is going on by just someone's face? Can you really tell the pain behind the smile?

They came back to see their mother, and I just happen to be there when they walked in the door. I never did understand what was going on till years later. The letters I got from my older sister I cherished them. I would read them over and over again. The sad part is I lost the letters in the box when I moved to Michigan in December.

My ancestors were seafaring and a warrior race that had sailed many of the same seas while I was in the U.S. Navy. They were both sailor and a very fierce warrior who had pushed out of Norway in search of new lands and riches. I had thought about that as I was getting ready to enter the U.S. Navy and how I was the first of my immediate to join the Navy as I had seen a lot of my other family had joined the Army and one brother went into the Air Force. You could say I wanted my own land and riches in joining the Navy, but for me that was a better life than the one I was now enjoying. I later learned my nephew was in the navy to and we were stationed in the same area.

America had been attacked by an enemy that is bent on the destruction of the American way of life. It is an enemy that has been at war for 1000's of years with the Christian world. Israel is a country that has been at war with its enemies such as Syria, Iran, Iraq, and the Palastein for 1000's of years. America supports Israel against its enemies that want to destroy Israel. Spain was a point of conflict with the Muslim world.

The Muslim people had a foot hold in Spain till driven out and back across the sea. The Muslim world not happy set their sights on the Byzantine Empire which was one beacon of the Christian world. Now America being prospers supporter of human rights and Israel. One time America supported Bin Laden in his conflict with Russia but in time things always change.

One the thing that has changed in the conflict of two ideological worlds was the weapons that are being used to kill with. That it will be a long war on terror and that we will win no matter how long it took, President Bush said standing there on the ruble of ground zero twin towers of the World Trade Center.

One big thing sets thing that sets Al Qaeda, like the Viet Kong, a part from the United States. Does America really understand the enemy that they are facing because they are a society that has been at war and conflict for 1000's of years. They embrace death as if it was a path to saint hood for them. America has been changed ever since 9/11 but has things really changed.

The Connie was on its way home from the cruise and on the news the family members, friends and the entire crew watched the attacks unfold on the news. No one could believe what they were seeing on television as it was unfolding in real time. The government couldn't rap there head but yet the Government knew they needed to figure out what was going on. Where the country would be attacked next and that is why they grounded and suspended all air travel. Things were happening and unfolding at a fast pace.

It did give rise to a lot of rumors as to what would be the role of the Connie since it was still at sea. It was the lack of communication from the top to the bottom that gave rise to those rumors that was going on the Connie. When we did get home off of cruise we were still subject to recall even though we were allowed to go on post cruise leave.

America Has been keeping their eyes on the Muslim world and patrolling the waters that are surrounded by the Muslim world. Some of the countries with in the Muslim world America support and help militarily. The first Desert Strom changed the way America operated overseas. One change was that No-fly zones in the North and South of Iraq were created that the United States Military patrolled. It also had changed the way U.S. Navy conducts its cruises, which has East and West coast carriers patrolling in the Persian Gulf, which is a change in the normal Med. Cruise.

United States felt like that it needed to end Saddam Hussens rein. Lots of countries did not support the war in Iraq. It was a war in a lot of ways the military did not expect when the war started. What happened after the conflict and objects were met were not expected and I don't think they expected what did happen. Which was a lightening entrance to Baghdad and removal of Hussen, which shows how well trained and armed the United States military is. Violence broke out and looting took place at the palaces and lot of the government buildings, but the military and the government was not prepared for it.

Americans say they are tired of war because they are not in the war to win it unlike the extremists of Islam. They are in this fight with America to win the fight and they won't tire or back away until they win the fight.

Back when they fought with sword, axes, spears and shields, they used to say to the warrior going into battle come back with your shield or on it.

"Always Aware: The journey of my life" was the first book I published about my life, and now I am adding more about my life in this book I titled "Taking Charge". I wrote this book because I wanted to share my struggles,

3

sadness and how I overcame those struggles. I had to take charge of my life, and move forward with creating the life that I wanted. A journey can take you too many different places and you can learn many different things on that journey. Your life is nothing but a series of journeys.

The struggles have led me to want more for my life. I went back to college, so I could work toward that better life that I wanted. I never gave up on getting my business degree which I received in August of 2011 while continuing to work toward a degree in Computer Drafting and Design. Real estate is part of that better life that I want for myself. I wanted to do something I love after all the back breaking and hard work and endless jobs I had done.

I took charge of my life, hence the title of the book, to make a better life for myself. That better life has started with going back to college and getting my real estate sales person license. I have combined this with my college studies, so I could see how a house is built and designed. They say knowledge is power and knowledge and understanding of the real estate, housing and building industry.

After the collapse in the financial industry I started gaining knowledge and investing in the

stock markets. Loans have been hard to come by since the collapse and jobs have been lost since then. What I have learned about finances I wrote down in my second book that I published a few months ago. The name of the book is "Olsen: My financial journey. I also like to teach students about finances and what I have learned about finances. I started a Financial Literacy Foundation LLC since my mother has passed away. My mother, Viola Olsen, liked to help the teachers and help the school.

Chapter 1

Growing up in New Plymouth, ID

~ § ~

It was a chilly winter day in January that I was born to Albert and Viola on the 28th of 1960. My older sister Marilyn and older brother Larry helped give me my name. Mom had let Larry and Marilyn go and visit their father, and that was the last I would see of them for some years. I was just about one year when that happened. Early on in my life I had gotten a red wagon for Christmas, but then there was this one day that I had pulled my little red wagon across the road behind me. There was this motorist that had to stop for me, and took me back the house and told my mom what I had done. My mom had been working on a western shirt that day she has never finished to this day.

I was just but a normal little kid growing up. I was an active child that had a very vivid imagine to match. Seeing my dad get ready for work early in the morning as I watched him eat breakfast as my mom prepared his lunch for him to take with him. I had seen my dad finish his breakfast as he got up from his chair; he picked up his lunch as he kisses mom good-bye and headed off for whatever lay ahead for him that day. I had watched him leave from the doorway before I returned to the living room, and got ready to watch cartoons like Aqua man, Superman, the Monkeys and the Beatles.

I watched cartoons such as Space ghost, The Banana Splits, Scobby Doo and the Vulture Squadron growing up. I remember teaching my little brother, along with my younger sister Anita, on how to crawl out of the play pen mom used to keep us kids in, while she did stuff in the kitchen. We crawled in and over the side of the play pen till Donald could climb out of it on his own. I finally got to meet Charles Mom's oldest son for the first time, I finally got to see Larry and Marilyn again. Then they were gone again and I wouldn't get to see any of them till later on in my life. I didn't know what was going all I knew they came in the door and then they were gone again. We were a melted family growing up so there was always a brother and sister coming and going. I didn't truly know what was going on so I just accepted as a normal part of my life.

It was my first day in the first grade and mom seen to it that I made it to the right class room. I sat there in class listening to Mrs. Noel speak to the class. She said that we would be there all day, and then all I remember getting that uneasy feeling about that cause it was the first I had really been away from home. I got scared and thought I would never see home again. I did later learn there was a certain time that we did get out of school. It was a few days later when they started a new first grade class and they were looking for volunteers to move into this new class, and I was one of the kids that volunteered for the class. Miss Meeker became my new first grade teacher instead of Mrs. Noel.

There were too many kids who rode the bus that my sister and I rode. That one bus dropped off and picked up kids from a set route. To alleviate the overcrowding on the bus, the driver split the route into two parts, and Diane and I had to wait at the school for the bus driver to come back and pick us up. We played on the monkey bars, the slide, merry-go-round, and swings while we waited for the bus driver to come back and get us. It did take us awhile before we finally got home from school. I had crawled off the side of the slide a few times and jumped down on to the ground, but this time when I did I slipped and fell to the ground. The small of my back it a bar that held the slid up, and I had to be taken to see the nurse that. I had a sore back that night.

Christmas was coming soon and I had been looking through the Christmas catalogs from Sears and Montgomery Ward. I would make a list of the toys that I wanted for Christmas. Mom brought home the tree, and then we all got to decorate our Christmas tree. Dad would make sure the tree was straight first before we got to decorate it. The tree decorating was done ahead of the holiday and then was taken down the day after New Year's. There was this one particular where I had found out where my parents had hidden all of our Christmas presents. So that year, I knew what I was getting for Christmas that year. Our dinner consisted of either ham or turkey along all the trimmings and then for desert apple and pumpkin pies. Christmas each year was pretty much the same, but the only difference we may have ham one year and then the following we would have turkey.

I remember asking my mom one day as to what my dad actually did for a living because we didn't see him much due to the time constraints that would only let him are at home with his family isn't the evenings. and some time he had to spend some nights at work in a sleeper car. I remember my mom telling me that he worked for the Union Pacific Railroad as a carpenter. When the weather got bad out or we just got bored Anita, Don, and me would take are tricycles, and ride them in a circles around the inside of the house for hours on end just for something to do. Dad was gone off to work those days, so he could not see do it. I am sure we would have gotten in trouble if he would have caught us riding the tricycles in the house.

Getting older and heading off to school where the learning continued to expand as my imagination grew. Drawing on some of lifes lessens that I had already been exposed to earlier in my life. Are minds are always growing and expanding as we learn more as life goes on. This was my early introduction to the career world as I watched my dad head of to work, and he could earn that paycheck to keep his family in the basic needs and necessities of life. Seeing dad leave so I continued on being a kid after I seen him leave. Playing as a kid will play and continue to be an active kid, and I continued to explore my world and learn. With my Lincoln logs and legos I would build houses, walls and as tall a building for as many legos I had to work with. Then I always put my construction to the test to see if it could with stand the things a kid throw at it.

Those days when dad did got the chance to spend time at home with us mainly in the evenings. Those days were few and far between that he got to spend time at home with us kids. As a family, we did cherish those days that we did have are dad at home with us. I used to see him take the time to read a book. He loved to read a good western by Louis L'Amour or even a Reader Digest condensed books.

My fourth grade teacher was Mrs. Neilson. It would be the first organized sport I would participate in, but I wasn't big on watching it on television. It was the first time I really had played basketball. It was my first basketball practice and the couch had us line up to shot free throws. My shots didn't even come close of hitting the basket. I didn't give-up on playing and trying to learn how to play better. I still made it to the practices and the games on Saturdays which had lasted for about three months. My first crush was for a girl named Anna she was a tall gal with brown hair. She invited to go with her to the Mormon Church, but my mom told me I couldn't go. The next year she had moved away, and I didn't see her again.

Cary and Allen showed me how to make what they called a popper. A few of us continued to play with them even though recess was over with. The teacher had started to teach class, and she wanted the noise to stop. I was one that didn't stop and was not paying attention to the class because I thought the popper was more fun to play with. The disruption continued till one of us got in trouble and that person was Cary who had got caught. He told the teacher he didn't do it, but Mrs. Neilson was not to be persuaded out of it. I didn't speak up and tell her that I was doing it, but was I the only one that continued to play.

There could have been other as well, because I wasn't looking around to see what was going on. The called Cary to the front of the class, and then she went across the hall to get Mrs. Anderson to witness the paddling. Mrs. Anderson stood there and watched as Mrs. Neilson delivered the spanking to Cary's bottom. It was the end of the year and the sporting events were at hand. I did participate and i did hold my own in the ones I chose to participate in. It was at the end of the school year we got to participate it a few different sporting games such a three legged race and lots other races, and pass and punt the football.

Dad need to go to his brother Ole's place, and on the way we stopped by Lowell's Mini Mart. Dad bought himself a Coke while I waited for him in the car. Dad offered me a drink of his Coke as he stepped away, but I drank more than a sip. He never did get mad or raise his voice about it but I could see he was frustrated with what I had done.

Beatrice, Grandma, as we referred to her, she lived on Dearborn Street, which was kind of a busy street. The house was a one-story house with a basement. Grandma's house sat on a double lot. Grandma worked part time for the McClure's bakery in Caldwell. She also baby-sit the Upson kids during the week. My aunt's kids lived down the street. I got to play with them when we would visit my Grandma, and sometimes we would even walk down to my aunt's house to play. My aunt's house was a smaller house. Grandma wore dresses that she had made. They were light in colors with small prints for the designs on the material.

She kept a hanky with her to wipe her nose with. She enjoyed working on quilts with the other women from the church. One day while we were staying with my grandma while my mom was at church camp for the week. I had gotten caught lying to her, and as my discipline I got a spanking with a wooden paint spatula. The biggest reason I lied to her was that I scared about what I had done and embarrassed as well. I did get upset about getting a spanking from my grandma, but I later got over it. I had always respected my grandmother even though the visits got fewer as the years past bye. Looking back now on it though, I can I deserved the spanking and I should have never lied to my Grand-ma but I was also a young kid who thought he would get in trouble if he had told the truth about it. I ended up getting in trouble for it any way wither I told the truth or not.

My brother and sisters and I sat down each and every week to watch Batman. My dad happened to be home when I started to act out one of the programs scene. I didn't hit my older brother but I did throw punches and a few kicks at him. Well because I acted out my dad banned us from watching the program any more. We did get to watch it now and then while dad was out taking care of business he had to take care of.

It was the first day of school and the start of a new year. It was then I had noticed that the girl I had a crush on had moved away. I was now in the 5th grade now, and Mrs. Wilson was my teacher. I tried out for the little league football team, but I really didn't get to play though. I made it to all of the practices after school let out for the day. Even then I didn't stand out from the rest of the players on the team. It was still the competing against the other players on the team, and against the players from the other teams we competed against. I tried out for the school band that year. I wanted to try and play the drum. The music teacher had us learn how to play the flute and kazoo and sing for a concert the school would put on.

We had to buy the flute and the kazoo we needed to play. Winter time was upon us and the basketball season was about to start and it was time to put your name on the list if you wanted to play. I practiced hard and I played the way I practiced and I gave it all I had. I managed to score a few points and I had stolen a few balls during a few games. That summer I tried out for the little league baseball team. I made it to all the practices even though I wasn't the best of players. I still tried hard during all of the practices. I didn't get to play in any of the games, but I still contributed to the team as the first base coach. We had a good run that season, but it ended in heart break. We lost the playoff game that ended the season for the team.

One day George and I were outside playing baseball together, and we also played touch football that could get a little rough at times. I was bating and George was pitching to me. I missed the first pitch and then he threw the ball once more. When George pitched the baseball to me, but this time he would plunk me in the side of the head with the baseball. He did yell at me but like the time he threw the rock my way. I didn't duck out the way of the ball. I would drop the bat spelling the end to that fun. The snow came and so did the touch football games in the snow with George. Neither one of us won any of the games that we played.

The second lesson I learned in these early years was how important family was to the both of them. They always tried to find time to spend with their brothers and sisters, and sometimes there were those days that got tougher. The economy and situations in life that can make things tougher to keep in touch with the rest of the family. Sometimes life throws lots of challenges a persons way making it tougher to try and stay close with the extended family. We did live far apart from each, and economics did play a part weather family got to see each other. I remember as a little kid I had a liking for the Vikings, so as I got a little older I had got the chance to talk with my Grandma Hoyt more about are heritage and she told in are family that we did have a relative that was a real Viking. A story of my Viking ancestors my grandma might have told me.

The Norwegians are a proud people and proud of their Viking past, and shared their past exploits with the others. Ole the Viking raider from the north who rained terror upon the unsuspected English, Scotsman, Irish and Italian populations. They plundered their wealth for their own. His group of open long ships came upon an English village in the north of England. When they had landed on the shore, they could see the village off a little ways. They leaped out of the ships, grabbed their weapons and shields.

Ole and his men began their journey toward the frightened English village. The villagers ran in fear of their life as they encountered the Viking raiders. Their fate was in the hands of the Vikings they encountered. The fierce battle raged on with the villagers. The battle ended with the wealth of the villagers being plundered by Ole and his men. They returned to their village in Norway. As they entered the mouth of the fjord, they could see all the people on the pier. Ole and his men were met at the pier by his wife, his family, and all the villagers.

They returned to the family farm where he shared what had happened with the rest of his family. He also showed them what he had brought back with him from England. Ole spent some time taking care of the family farm. Later that year when the time was right Ole and his men met in the long house where they started planning their next raid. After some discussion, plans were made, and the meeting broke up. The outcome the meeting was a raid on Italy and they had decided to carry out the raid in two days.

They waved good-bye to their families as they departed on their journey. The men rowed away from the pier, and once they have cleared the mouth of the fjord. They hoisted their sail and nod now with the wind filling their sail. Now that they were on their way they charted their course for the coast of Italy. They had seen a sail off in the distance. They altered their course to attack the merchant ship at sea, and losing none in the attack. They resumed their course for Italy. The ship flexing as the waves break over the bow of the ship and the salt water of the waves hitting the men.

The ships cutting through the waves on its way to a village, that was near the coast in south of Italy. Once they had arrived at their destination, Ole and his men quickly offloaded the ship and were making their way across the beach toward the meeting point. Now that the men were gathered to gather they made their way to the village that lay over the mountain and through the woods. Shields up in fighting and with swords drawn, Ole and his men stormed the Italy town. The villagers were falling at the ends of the swords of ole and his men. The last of villagers have and the treasures have been loaded on the ships. Ole and his men weighed anchor and headed for their home in Norway.

On their way home, they saw another sail at sea. They altered their course to attack, arrows filled the sky, the merchant ship at sea, the ships protecting the merchant ships. Under a hail of arrows, the attacking ships neared their target. Grappling hooks dragging the ships nearer, Ole and his men jumped over to the other ships with swords, axes and shields in hand, while they attacked the ships. During the ensuing battle ole was killed. The riches were transferred to Ole's ships along with Ole and his men's bodies. They returned home to their village with their dead.

The following year of school I did have an interest in playing little league football that year. I did make all of the practices after school, and I did try as hard as I could during the practices. I didn't get to play much in any of the games, but I didn't give up. I still continued to practice till the end of the football season. My dad had a job to do one weekend, and he had decided to take me along with him. I was to help him out on the job site. One by one digging began along with the setting of each of the fence posts, but to ensure the fence posts were straight. My dad showed me how to string what he referred to as a singing wire.

This was how dad was going to ensure the fence posts were lined up in a straight line. Now with that in place we started to set each of the posts into place. I helped my dad by holding each of the boards in place as dad nailed them to the posts. I hand dad a 2x4 that he weaved in the middle of the boards that he had just nailed to the posts. After the job, we loaded all of the tools once the job was complete, and set out for home. I decided to try and play basketball my 6th grade year, and I did pretty good. My 6th grade school year had come to an end and now it was time to advance to the 7th grade.

I had been watching movies, like "The Vikings" starring Kirk Douglas and Tony Curtis, and programs that had castles sieges and the defenders trying to repel the siege. I didn't have much to do, so I got the idea to make some arrows and a bow from the limbs I had trimmed from the trees in the front yard. Knife in hand I whittled a point to the branches to make my arrows, and a few notches so I could string my bow. Now that I had them made I walked to the backyard. I pictured the roof of the garage as my castle, so I climbed on to the roof. I crawled on my hands and knees to the roofs edge with bow and arrows in my hands. Stringing the arrows on to my bow I fired at the attackers. The attackers being Anita and Donald who was walking toward me, and it kind of scared them cause they had no idea what was going to happen. It didn't last but a few seconds and was over.

I knew some of the story about my brothers and sister but I would not know the whole story till years later. I never could see the pain and heart ache in my mom's face or even in my dad's face. They never did let on to what was going on in their life as they also had their hands full with the kids that they had from their union which is George, Diane, John, Anita and Donald.

I started asking mom about Marilyn and asking her different question about her. Mom also explained to me at that time what had happened and I also asked if I could write to her. Mom gave me her address and I wrote to her a few times. I kept those letters and reread them many times. Mom had also told me a few times that Larry was coming home for a visit but something always happened that prevented him from coming home to visit. I tried to understand the best I could but could I really understand what was going on and had happened. I also had mom take some pictures of me that I sent to my sister Marilyn.

My older sister did come home after she had graduated college with a nursing degree. She made it home in time for Diana and Jon Martin's wedding. Mom, her daughter Marilyn and I, Mom drove us around Nyssa, OR looking at different thunder eggs before we paid a visit with Diana and her husband. It was a fun time visiting with them before we headed back home.

Even early on as well in later life I was made to feel as if I didn't fit in or was different from the others in my class. I was always true to myself by being nice to those around me even though some days that was hard. There was this particular day I had went to school after I had received this peace sign patch from my sister Marilyn and then had it sowed on this old army shirt that I liked to wear as a jacket to school. She had sent me that patch after she had went back home after her visit. That patch got stolen from me while I was in one of my classes. One thing I had learned was to always treat people the way that you would like to be treated, but even at that I was still always picked on and had things stolen from me. Then there was those days that I had to even stand up for my own self cause I had enough of getting picked on and by todays standard I could have got charged with assault for getting in a fight.

I played basketball, but didn't get to play much during the regular games. I did keep showing up, and trying to do the best of my ability that I did have. I wrestled, and I did win a few of my matches against opponents from Fruitland, Homedale, and Parma. One of my favorite classes in the 7th grade was the art class taught by Mrs. Beale. I wasn't the best of drawers but it still taught me a lot about what I do like to draw. I did ok in track that year, but I got to being lazy and I skipped a lot of the practices. That led me to being kicked off the team before they went to district. My first job that spring was mowing lawn for Mr. and Mrs. Christiansen, and then I picked up mowing lawns for Dr. Davis, Mrs. Bradley, and Mrs. Robanet. My lawn mowing business was steadily growing over the next few years.

The following year I tried out for the football team and was doing pretty well until I started chasing a girl and skipping football practices. Mr. Beale had talked to my mom about playing football. He still wanted me to play, and I tried to get things going again. It was too late in the season. It ended their shortly their after. I went on to play basketball, and wrestle. I did pretty well in both of them. I went out for track and had a whole lot more success this time around because I stuck with it and didn't skip out on the practices this time.

I won the first race in the first track meet of the season. I came out of the blocks running hard and fast for the whole race, but I still almost lost it in the end because I came out hard and too fast. My team mates cheered for me and pushed me on to the win. That was to be my one and only win for the rest of the season, but I still finished pretty respectable. I finished in the top 5 finishers in the 660 yard race at the Payette county championships and in 7th place in the 660 yard race at district. I still had some problems with some of my classroom work, and a lot of it wasn't applying myself to the school work. I did get bored in the classes as well but I could have done lots better if I just applied myself to my studies.

Jeff asked me if I wanted to help him with some work at the fairgrounds, and I agreed to help him. The work was to replace some of the bad boards in the bleachers of the Payette County Rodeo Arena. Mr. Hilton later called me up to see if I could help him with another project he had to do at the fairgrounds. Mr. Hilton was the care taker of the fairgrounds. I met him at their place, and from there we walked over to the fairgrounds. He showed me what needed to be done, and that was to replace the roof on the milk barn. The milk barn is where the 4-H show people milked out their cows that they were showing in the fair.

I picked up the hammer and nails, and started to nail 2x4's to the trusses of the barn. Mr. Hilton informed me that I was doing it wrong, and that I needed to stagger the joints of my 2x4's. He showed as he explained to me what I was doing wrong. I went about the job as Mr. Hilton went about things he had to take care of. Mr. Hilton came back to check on how I was doing. He then explained to me that Elvis had just passed away. Prices of food, clothes and gas were on the rise and we were feeling the effects of the rising prices. I had decided to make it my final year for mowing lawns cause of something's that happened at home.

It was also in these early I was exposed to the value of the dollar as I asked my mom for some to buy something as turns to me as tells we can't afford, so I remember thinking to myself that I want to get a job so I can afford whatever I wished to buy. As I got older and trying earning money by working so I can pay for things I wanted in those early years of my life. Not thinking of mowing lawns as a business but more as a way to earn money for the things I wanted. Gaining that experience to help me grow and broaden my horizons in my life. My early working life began with driving tractor for my uncle, as well bucking hay for him and others.

My uncle would have me stop the tractor, but every now and then I would accidentally pop the clutch and jerk the hay wagon. My uncle got unhappy when it happened but he didn't yell at me for it though because he knew I didn't mean to do it. Then moving on to mowing lawns, working for youth conservation corp, milking cows and moving sprinkler pipes for very little money to get by on. With the money I had earned from all my working I never really thought about saving, or even investing it for the future cause all I ever thought about was to spend it on whatever I wanted at the time. My mom tried to get me to save it but all I would ever do with it is blowing it. Cause with very little financial education at that time other then what you learn in school you just don't think about those things.

Mrs. Williamson called me up and wanted me to trim her trees up. I had told her that I quit mowing lawns and taking care of the yards, but she still wanted me to trim up the trees like I had the year before. The limbs on these trees had some big thorns on them, so if they stuck you it hurt. It is during the evenings we played Clue, Risk and Monopoly, and I was a pretty competitive player. World domination and having the money to build houses and hotels, so you could get more money is what appeal to me about Risk and Monopoly. They all took a lot strategy, luck to win the games.

The school guidance counselor thought I had a learning disability, so he made me an appointment with the vocational rehab counselor. The day came that I was to meet with the counselor and passing all of the tests. The counselor said from the results of the tests that there was nothing they could do for me cause I didn't meet there guidelines. I was pulled aside along with a group of other students to meet with some Marine corp recruiters. So from the advice, I was given I had considered leaving school early and joining the Marines. I had also considered going into the Navy as well. I had also talked to my friend Cynda about this and she thought it was the wrong thing for me, and had me promise that I would stay in school and graduate.

One day as I was helping my uncle Ole, I had over heard him talking about how the younger generation instead of saving and working for what they wanted but they wanted it all right now instead of waiting and taking there time. Taking there time and accumulate the pieces over time as you were able to afford them. My dad one day had told me about some pick pockets that could pick yours while they wore bells on there fingers, and if you heard the bells your pocket had been picked. That was just another reason for me to stay aware of my surroundings.

I had always enjoyed spending time and hunting with my sister Diane and her husband. Some days my brother-in-law would bring his friend around with him as we ether played a game of basketball or went hunting together. There was one particular day though that one of his friends turned to me and made the comment to me about how ugly I was and all I remember doing was standing and thinking to myself as to why he tell me such a thing.

Well another year ended and once again before the start of the new school year I had considered to quit school. Now after talking to Diane and her husband I went and applied for a job at the sugar beet factory, but my mom had other plans and that was for me to stay in school. Mom met with the guidance counselor and had enrolled me in school. Well back to school I went for another year.

It was another summer that was soon coming to an end, and knowing where I stood credit wise. I went to register for the up and coming school year, and I handed my class schedule to the guidance counselor. He then informed me that I would be held back a year, cause of the lack of credits I needed to graduate. So needless to say, I was disappointed about that, and that pushed me to try harder to graduate. During the year I had an interest in being a blacksmith and working with a forge, but I had to first get past arc wielding and acetylene wielding. It was at the end of the year that I was the friendliest person in the class by my classmates in the "class on 79". That was weird because it was some of the ones in the class that used to pick on me and have stolen some things from me.

It was during my final year of school that decisions had to be made on whether I was going to go to college an what I was to major in. It was with the help of the guidance counselor. I decided to pursue a degree in wielding. He had discouraged me from taking a major that had a lot of math with it. I wanted to try my hand at rodeoing, and during the summer I had registered for the rodeo. I had took a look at Treasure Valley Community College and decided to attend and to pursue a major in raising horse as well as rodeoing.

One day talking to My dad he told that he wish he could have sent me to this ranch he knew of, But he wasn't sure that they were still there though. Then my dad proceeded to tell me that i wouldn't amount to much and that my little brother would amount to more then i would. I remember thinking to myself after that I was going to set out to prove to him that I could succeed and truly become something. As well you might say as to prove what he had just would be wrong.

Sometimes the work was time consuming and very back breaking that paid usually less then minimum wage at the time. Yet I persevered and always tried to complete the job at hand and in a timely manner. I remember thinking to myself that there must be a better job out there for me. Saving my money up for the summer, and as fall neared I had plans of heading of to school. I could get a degree, and a better job that came with that degree. I decided on a degree in Horse Production.

My first day of classes I had met this cute blond gal and I remember thinking to myself that I would love to get to know her lots better to. I did get to know Virgina lots better but I never did get to know her much more than as friend. I hung out at college playing pool against fellow students, while we talked to each other between classes. Then again after class was over I went over to a fellow classmate's place where I had a few drinks and played tag football with my new classmates. It was there I got to hanging out with Virgina some more at a gathering after rodeo practice.

It was at college that I first met the women that would later I would marry. I had seen and talked with her a few other times around campus. It wasn't until I went to college that I was first exposed to building and running a business, and thinking about a business in raising horses. I had been around cattle most of my life from the time I could walk as I had grown up on a farm. Pursuing a academic and social life in college as there you meet lots of people from all different backgrounds and walks of life. One of lifes challenges though was the money needed to pursue a college degree as it had ran short, and back to work I went. The one thing still eludes me to this day for all the hard work is that college degree. I had to put the goal on hold yet again for that dream job that had eluded me yet once more.

I was now broke, and I decided to go back to work on the farm for the summer. Then from there I had gone to work for a print shop in the back of a newspaper office after I had been let go from Holms Dariy farm. I had continued rodeoing so during my stay at the office I had got interviewed for an upcoming column about the local rodeo that was coming soon to town. Mark a newspaper reporter, ex-student and student body president at Treasure Valley Community College. I had met him the year before at the college.

While I was working there I had saved up some money to go back to college for another semester, but I also knew I would have to go back to work again. My mom went and got her son my older brother Larry from the VA hospital and brought him home to live with us. I was just a little kid when I had seen him last. His life had been shaped by his father and the hell of war in Vietnam. I wouldn't know what his life, his brother and sister's life was like until years later. The things would have been different if we wouldn't have been robbed of a life together as brothers that had grown up together.

I went back to work on the farm setting water, and then later I was asked if I wanted to milk the cows. While I had been working on the dairy farm, I decided to buy a few calves now and then to raise. Treating and raising the calves as a business for myself, while I was still working on the farm. My next business step was to apply for a cattle brand from the State Brand inspector. Now after I had gotten my brand from the state. I then paid a visit to the local blacksmith shop to have them make me a couple of branding irons for my business.

I finally received my branding irons from the blacksmith. I now could brand the first of my calves that were old and big enough to be branded. It was one night after work that I had decided to go out to the bar to just relax that night, but I ended up running into Della that I had met in college along with some other of her friends. I hadn't seen her for several years before that night. We just talked and danced till late into the night. The days and months flowed by as we continued to see a lot more of each other as I continued to work on the dairy farm and raise a few calves on the side.

So treating it as a business, I would sell the calves after the brands on the calves had healed. The calves were hauled to the auction ring in Weiser, ID to be sold at auction. That way I could show an income against my expenses for a write off against my income taxes. I helped my dad build a shelter for the calves to keep out of the elements. I got help from my dad in building a separate pin for the heifer I had bought, and that way she didn't get bullied by the bigger calves I had. I had also attached an ear tag to each one of my calves besides branding them all.

Now as time had went by things had gotten a lot more serious with my girlfriend, and one night when were alone I took the opportunity to propose to her that night. The two of us together told family and friends a few days later that we were going to get married. Now we had plans to make, rings to buy, and to find a place for us to live in after we were married. For the honeymoon, we had use of this cabin on the lake for a week. I had decided to leave a few days early, and it was a good thing because my car had broken down on the way out of town. Later after we returned home the honeymoon that we got moved into our new apartment.

A few short weeks later after we moved in, we started getting visits from her cousin needing a place to sleep off his drunk. I had also taken her cousin to work with me on the farm every once in a while. Feeling the stress and tension at home and in the air I tried to balance work with raising a few calves while maintaining a home life. Even though I tried hard to make things work, but the struggles of it all were taking it toll on me.

This is when I had come to the conclusion that things had to change for me. So as a distraction, I took an opportunity to spend one last pheasant-hunting trip with my sister, brother-in-law and my new wife. It would be the last time I would go hunting with them since we went about our own separate lives. I wanted a change in jobs, and shortly after that I decided to join the naval service to see the world. I decided to enlist with the US Navy because I was tired of the life on the farm, and wanted more out of life. I then had to meet with the navy recruiter to fill out the necessary paper work along with all the tests they required.

I was also hoping to gain the necessary new skills that I could use later on in my life. I got to spend my birthday with most all of my family before I left for boot camp. I had also kept my cattle raising business going while I was away. The day came for me to leave for boot camp, and they had me stay in a hotel the night before. My wife was with me, and in the morning we decided to drive to the recruiting station, but on the way there the truck had broke down. Needless to say, I had to find a ride to get me where I had to go.

It was after I had arrived that I was processed and had to wait for a ride to the airport to fly out to San Diego, CA for boot camp. While waiting I got to spend the last few hours before I had to leave for boot camp with my mom and mother-in-law as well. Once arriving in San Diego, CA, I was met at the airport by a bus that was there to take all new recruits to the Navy boot camp base. Once I had arrived at the base we were to taken to this building where we were processed in. Then after being processed in we were sent to the holding barracks for a few nights. There I was joined with other fellow recruits for the first of many urinalyses tests. It took me a while to get the test done to.

Chapter 2

Boot Camp

~ § ~

That first night lying there asleep in those barracks as time felt like it passed by very quickly as we were awaken long before the sun had come up. The silence of the night was broken by the sound of them beating on a garbage can. That first night felt like it passed by very quickly before we were rudely awaken to the beating of the garbage can. Looking outside of the barracks all I could see was a pitch black sky as we hurried to get dressed for the start of long day. The other recruits that the command put in charge of us woke us up and took the awaiting company to the galley for breakfast. Finishing breakfast quickly we returned to the barracks at which time we were picked up by our company commander. Standing there in front of as he introduced himself to us.

There shortly after the intros were finished colors begun to play over the load speakers. Shortly thereafter, we had to learn how to march as a group. The drills continued till we were sent to lunch, and following lunch we marched to get are first issue of uniforms. After we got our issue of uniforms we marched to the barracks stowing our gear we marched to dinner. Following dinner we were returned to the barracks for the night. Once again we were rudely awakened but this time it was our Company Commander wakening us up before the sun had come out. We formed up and we all marched to the parade ground and then on to breakfast. We had to eat breakfast quickly and then reform up in the spots that we marched to breakfast in.

This morning was different because now we were in are Navy uniforms and now we all looked the same as any other recruit in the Navy. I followed out some people who I thought was from my company, but I quickly realized that they weren't from my company. Now I tried to find my company but in a sea of blue and it being pitch black didn't make it easy. Whether it was right or not I made my way back to the barracks to await their return since I had gotten separated from my company. I made my way past the guards at the bridge who were recruits themselves and made my way back to our barracks where I waited the return of my company. Once I had seen I had seen from the barracks window my company had returned. I walked out from the barracks to rejoin them on the grinder. I could see on my company commander that he was not happy with me, but he didn't punish us over it ether. I thought I did what was right that day under the given circumstances of being lost and separated from my group.

Long before the sun had come up we were woke up by our company commander, and dressing quickly we were formed up in a height line, before we formed up in formation as marched to breakfast. Having eaten we quickly reformed up in formation to be taken to receive are first are first shots, and haircuts before we were taken to lunch. Having eaten lunch were taken to the building where we received are initial outfitting. Reforming up with are duffel bags in hand before we returned to the barracks, and putting up are stuff before we were sent to dinner.

Morning came before the sun came up as we headed for breakfast and then off to the pool for are swimming test. Having jump in and trying to swim but not making it past the first attempt I was helped out of the pool. I needed some extra guidance to help me pass the test while I was in boot camp. Half the company went outside to spit shining their boon dockers, while the other half shit, showered and shaved. Then the half that was spit shining their shoes now were shit, showering and shaving while the others were now spit shining their boon dockers outside the barracks.

The company's preparatory days were coming to an end. We stood there before the reviewing stand a newly formed company before being lead to breakfast that early chilly morning. We had to quickly eat breakfast before we returned to the barracks, and gather up our gear for the move into our new home away from home for the next eight weeks. Following the weekend started the classroom studies as the continued drilling with the physical exercises. During that first week we had taken a reading comprehension test. I would learn the results of my first dental check-up, and it was not good.

I had to have a lot of work done to my teeth as a result of my bad habit and neglect of my teeth. I had missed the test score cutoff by a very slim margin, and as a result of missing the cut off by .01. I got setback for several weeks, where I had received help with my reading skills. I had often wonder why I had gotten set back that day along with other recruits that had chosen not to go to dinner that night. One by one we were called into the Company Commanders office and told that we were being sent to a special barracks where they were going to give us help with our reading. We were told to gather our stuff up and report there in the morning.

Meanwhile I was away, I had gotten a letter from my mom telling me one of my calves had died and that the other calf had gotten out Mom told that the calf was over at the neighbor's house in there pins. I wrote to my wife to go get the calves and to take them up to her grandmas till I was able to get back home to take care of them. I had finally passed the remedial reading class after which I was sent to meet up with my new company commander and the others I would be with for the next eight weeks.

I met my new Company Commander CPO (Signalman) Kovar at where my new company was at uniform issue. He made me pull out all my uniforms and clothes one by one, and restencil them with my new company number, but I had to cross out the old company number. Having been set back to the preparatory days I had to retake my shots and the swim test I had passed earlier. The reading test that had gotten me before, but this time I had passed it. The days were filled with classes, drilling and physical exercising as we studied for are classes after dinner. We received our next outfitting before we had gone to lunch.

One night Chief pulled me aside to escort Dave to medical hold, and once at medical hold with him. I told the person in charge I was here because I was asked to escort Dave to medical hold, and once done I made my way back to the barracks. We had just returned from breakfast when I noticed Dave had made his way back to the barracks. People in charge of medical hold came to the barracks after Dave, but as soon as they got there he ran. Later that we marched across a bridge that crossed a river that ran through the boot camp and training command. I looked off to the west where I had noticed some foot prints in some sand like someone tried to run up the side of the river bank. I figured it was Dave trying to escape the people who were after him. I am sure he was caught and processed out of the Navy.

The many challenges of the days ahead like the gas and smoke house. They instructed how the gas house was to go and what we were to do while we were in the gas house. We broke up in to different groups and finally it was my groups turn to enter the gas house. Once in the gas house we lined up in front of the instructor's in charge of gas house. They instructed us to remove our masks and hold them over our head. Now they instructed my group to recite one of the ten general orders, and as a group we started to recite the requested general order. Well as I started to recite it I made the mistake of taking a breath and with the gas in the air now. It made it very hard for me to say anything and now once outside I was able to speak and my clothes were able to air out.

Over the next few weeks there was the smoke house to come. We talked to the group that had went to the smoke house before us and they told us that they couldn't get the smoke house lite. A lot us were hoping that they couldn't get it lite when we would have to go through it next week. The company loaded up on the buses and off to 32nd street where the smoke house was located. Once there we had to fight a couple real fires in a tank and then go through the smoke house that they couldn't get lite. Instead they had us fight pretend fires that could happen in a compartment on the ship. Ship board firefighting is no joke and we all took it very serious. I managed to pass the gas and smoke house.

All the lights were out in the barracks, but some of us were still up walking around. We could see out over the water that ran through the boot camp from our second floor barracks window. That night we could see a house boat on the water and there were people inside the house boat having a little fun on the water late at night. We had weekly test that we had to study for and pass tests on Naval History and other things that we needed to know about and to prepare us for a career in the U.S. Navy. The big thing we had to pass was the run at the end of boot camp which was 2 and ½ miles along with push-ups and set-ups. I ran into my prior company commander who I was not to talk to and as result of me doing that I had to do some push-ups as a punishment for speaking to him.

Finally graduation day had arrived as we passed by our love ones in are dress uniforms. I was able to spend graduation night with my wife, and had dinner with her and my mom. Della, my mom and I went to breakfast before we caught the bus to take us to the San Diego Zoo where we spent a good part of the day walking around the zoo. I had a four hour watch that morning, but after my watch I was able to me Della and my mom at RTC\ NTC command building before they had to catch there flight out the following day. We took a few pictures of the time we got to spend together. I had a week to go before I got shipped out to my next duty station. We were able to take it a little easier that week. We had a going away BBQ that was attended by the commanding officer and the executive officer of RTC. The night before we had to go our way we had to clean and wax the barracks as we had packed our stuff up.

Naval Aviation Apprentice School

Finally the day came for me to be transferred to my school, and having arrived at my new barracks for my assigned school. Quickly settling before I had to stand watches also meeting with other people this was to be our class for the next four weeks. Still having to march to and from classes along with physical training before classes, but in so many ways it feels like a continuation of boot camp. That is because it was designed as a continuation of boot camp. The only difference now I was able to get off of the base, go shopping and able to go to the galley to eat on my own. Our class studies consisted of naval aviation history and all phases and aspects of naval aviation.

Finally graduation day for the class came, and now it was time for us to receive our graduation certificate and our orders to our first command. We now had our orders in hand, and after we had said our goodbyes to the rest of our classmates. I was excepting to be sent to Naval Air Station Moffet Field in Alameda for my C-school, and then to VQ-1 in Guam. My orders had gotten changed, and now I was going to the *USS Ranger (CV-61)* in Bermerton, WA. I had put down Bermerton, WA as a place that I would like to go for my choices of duty stations, and plus the *USS Ranger (CV-61)* was a high priority fill billet is why my orders had gotten changed.

One during one of our class's one of my fellow shipmates got caught nodding off in class and he was forced to stand in the back of the class room. He had to pick up a tail hook and hold it over head for a period time before he was allowed to put it down and seat back down in his seat. At least once a week we had to attend exercises at least once a week before we had to go to class. Thing is in order to go to the exercises meant we had to give-up going to breakfast because they were both at the same time. Well one day I chose not to go to exercises and I think few other never did ether well that night we had together in the courtyard for or own end of the day mashing cause we didn't go to the morning exercises.

It was my first taste in how the military really works and how they put people where they are needed. We caught a cab to the airport with a few other classmates. We had talked amongst us and agreed once we got to San Francisco because we had a lay over there that we would met for coffee at the coffee shop, but once I checked in I found out I had no lay over between flights. I never seen my fellow shipmates again after that. I had to hustle through the airports to make my connections, and I could get home after I had been away in boot camp. I finally got home to be with my wife and the rest of family. I had also taken the opportunity to brand my calves as well. After the brands had healed, I had taken all the calves, but the heifer taken to the auction ring. Meanwhile, I had the heifer vaccinated by the local vet. It felt like the next two weeks passed by quickly for me to continue on to my first duty station aboard the *USS Ranger (CV-61)* in Bermerton, WA.

Transfer to the *USS Ranger (CV-61)*

The travel on the bus was long and very uncomfortable bus ride to meet the *USS Ranger (CV-61)* in Washington. I finally arrived at my first duty station I was processed in, and as soon as the paperwork was finished. I was sent to the barracks where I went through indoctrination and damage control training. I got to spend time with my wife's cousin and his wife and she helped me find a place to rent there. Della's cousin was stationed on one of the small boys that had been in dry-dock and was getting ready to go out for its sea trails and workups for deployment. It was a place that was within walking distance of the base and the ship as I had no car of my own to drive.

The instructors told us about the big main machinery room fire that happened while they were out on cruise, and then document holding space catching fire because of some hot work going on in the aft adjoining balk head. The heat from the hot work caught the paper on fire because they had no fire watch on the other side of the balk head. The fire was a very hard one to fight because the space was full of paper documents. I think they had to flood the space to put it out because there was no other way to put it out. Eleven shipmates lost their lives in the Main Space fire, and you could see the damage from the fire still when it was in dry-dock. A fellow shipmate who was there fighting the fire told the smoke from the fire was so bad that it obscured the view of the carriers island structure.

Soon my wife was to join me, but before she left she took the last of my calves to the sale ring. I spent my whole time on the Ranger as a fire watch because I had no department at that time that I belonged to. I was an unrated E-2 and I was searching for a rate from the moment I set foot on the ship, and one the first rates I had an interest in was to be an Aviation Anti-Submarine Operator, which meant I would get to fly as an air crewmen. The drawback though was my swimming skills and they were not very good. I had the officer in charge of the fire watches on my side and he was helping getting the stuff going and pushing it through. I found out later why he was because he was an AW Chief Warrant Officer, and I made him mad when I came to them changing my mind about being an AW and now I wanted to be an Aviation Electrician's Mate an AE. This meant I lost his support for me trying to get an "A" school, but I would still get into the "A" School that I wanted.

Now with the last of my calves gone, it was the last of my calf raising business. We walked almost every place in order to get around town and to get are groceries. I decided to rent a car once in a while but in order for me to do that. I needed to put down a security deposit, because I didn't have charge card for it. I also walked to work where I stood fire watch as the wielders worked on the ship. I was there with the wielders in case of a fire was started so that I could put it out. One day, I decided to try and build my credit, and in doing I applied for my first charge card at Nordstrom. I applied for many other cards and a jewelry account that I used to replace the wife's wedding set after she had lost her engagement ring.

I had been told that the ship had a few collisions with other ships through the years prior. They were with a few oil tankers that I had been told. I was a fire watch and we got to go to different parts of the ship that you would never see through the normal course of your duties on the ship. Well I got to see first-hand some of the damage to the ship that those collision had caused to the ship. They had to hit the ships pretty hard to have left damage on the inside bulkheads of the ship.

We spent ten days at sea putting the ship through various drills and exercises to see if the ship was ready to go back to sea, and also to find out what work still needed to be done on the ship. I had my general quarter station and it was the very low deck of one of the weapons elevators. Soon I was transferring to my "A" school in Millington, TN and I got to spend my last few weeks on the ship as part of the Weapons Department.

AE "A" School

I had decided on working as an aviation electrician's mate. I applied for an A school and by early summer I was off for Millington, TN. After having left, the *USS Ranger (CV-61)* I was on my way to move my wife home sand that way I could spend a couple of weeks down time visiting with family and friends before I was off to resume my naval duties in Millington, TN. Wishing my family and friend's bye before I went off to my "A" school because my leave was coming to an end soon. Arriving a few weeks later in Tennessee I checked in with the clerk on duty after arriving on the naval base. So after I finished the paperwork I was sent to my home away from home while I was going to school.

I had gotten permission quickly to wear civilian clothes beings I was coming to "A" School from the fleet, but in the mean time I had to stand watches while waiting for my class to form up. We still had some shipmates who wear civilian clothes even though they couldn't at that time. I even noted it in the watch log book, but the following watch would line it out so they shipmate wouldn't get in trouble for it. I still think the one who lined out my log book entries should have gotten in trouble as well. I never told the barracks person in charge but I still noted it because I never let it slid like other people did. I played by the rules as they were set up by the military.

I had to still stand watches in the heat of the summer while I still had to study for my classes. I studied the basics of aviation and the basics of electricity and electronics. I had taken Aviation apprenticeship classes, and I had thought that was enough to challenge Aviation fundamentals.

I ended up failing the challenge, and had to take the class. One thing I learned from the class was always protect my own ass, because nobody else was. One person my tell you to do something but if something goes wrong they will deny that they ever told you to do it.

I couldn't tighten the nut on the blot enough to line up with the hole to safety wire them. That is when I raised my hand and asked one the instructors what I should do since I couldn't get it to line up properly. I was told to try and loosen it some to see if that worked, but that made it to loose then. I left that way and safety wired it in place, and I knew it was wrong, and what the instructor told me to do didn't help any. He denied he told me to loosen the bolt, but he didn't tell me to safety wire in place. From there on there was a change in the way I did things even though I was told to do them a certain way.

I stayed after class for more help, but I still fell short in testing so was sent to barracks hold while I waited for orders to my next duty station. While I was waiting I had to manage a crew while we worked cleaning the barracks, but in my off time I spent my time in the gym lifting weights.

My days on the *USS Independence (CV-62)*

Finally getting my orders I was being sent to the *USS Independence (CV-62)* that was in the shipyard in Philadelphia, PA. The day arrived to depart, and with orders and package in hand. A guy, I met at "a" school, and I shared a cab ride to the airport. I was flying home to spend 30 day leave, which was great, after I been away for a few months. Before catching my Flight to Philly, I got to spend the last few minutes with my wife. My next duty station and my awaiting ship at the Philly Naval Ship Yard. Arriving in Philly after my time off I caught a cab to the base that took me to the ship. I had to walk into this building that was next to the ship to check in with the duty personal men. I hand him my records and orders so after checking in I was shuttled over to barracks that the ships company was staying in.

Having got settled in I took the rest of the night to relax before I started a new day at my next command. Waking up early the next I walked to the galley and ate breakfast before I had to catch the bus that took me to the ship. Having arrived at the ship I had to walk to my department where I was to work. That first day they put me to work chipping paint from the bulkheads and grinding the paint from the decks. Sometime later I was transferred to another division in the weapons department that was removing the old wiring and lights. After removing them, we then replaced the wiring and lights with new florescent lights but in the process. We had to cut holes in the lagging, and that way the lights could be wielded in place. Petty Officer Walker told me how many lights there could be for a junction and that, and off I was designing where to put the lights and junction boxes in each of the weapon mags. I was the one in charge of the crew and made sure they got installed right and that they all worked perfectly.

One of the first stories I was told about the ship was how a sailor had hung himself in one of the weapon elevator shafts. Well one day I was doing some work in the weapons mag on the lighting panel and as I was working I kept hearing noises from in the area of the elevator shaft. I knew there was no one else working in and around where I was working, but I kept working on what I was doing. I heard the noises again, but this time I decided to take a look and see if there was any one around where I was that could be making the noises and as I got closer to the elevator shaft the noises stopped. When I walked away from the elevator shaft the noises started up again but this time I didn't go look and I just finished my work and left the weapons mag. Sometime later I heard other shipmates saying, they also had heard strange noises coming from that same elevator shaft and there was no one around to make the noises that they heard.

While I was away from home I got several phone calls from one of my creditors because they hadn't received a payment for four months. They wife hadn't sent them a payment cause she had combined the payments together. I had to work hard to get them caught up with the payments by even borrowing money to help. I had sent her the majority of my money to make the payments. I had decided one night after I had gotten the calls from Sears.

I made some other calls to some other creditors and found out Sears was not the only credit card that had not received any payments for what was owed. I was also sent down to the galley where I worked at keeping the tables clean and setting up my area with milk and juice for the meals. Halfway through time there I was sent to serve and help prepare the food for the crew's meals. Meanwhile, I studied my aviation electrician manuals because I never gave up on being an aviation electrician. That way I could make rank and more money. I had finally made rank after it had taken me four tries at taking the test. I had met up with an AO who had been transferred to the ship from the *USS Forrestal (CV-59)* and he told me about a lot of strange happenings on the ship. One story he told us is how people would get locked in the weapon mags they had unlocked to go to work in. They knew there was no one around when they went into the space, but somehow they just had gotten locked in the space.

Next he told me how strange figures could be seen in and around the storage freezers where they stored the dead bodies of the sailors that were killed in the fire and explosions that happened in the Gulf of Tonka which is of the coast of Vietnam. The freezers they stored the bodies in have since have been sealed and no longer being used for food storage. He also told me that people had seen people just standing there with old flight deck gear on. They were spotted there by the people on night watch and the watches went over to check them out. They saw a figure dressed in old deck gear, but with a closer look they looked like a spirit of a person.

After a few phone calls, to the detailers, and I could get some orders off of the ship. Finally receiving orders to Jacksonville, FL I was ready to depart for home after having been gone for a long time. I could see several ships moored at the end of this one pier, and one of the ships was a battleship that would be later towed down to dry docks in Mississippi to be brought back out of the moth ball fleet of ships. It was to retro fitted with state of the art equipment and missiles. It was to be part of the President Reagan ship build up that he had ordered.

Transfer to Naval Air Station Cecil Field, Florida

Time had been passing by quickly after I had been home for almost thirty days before I had to leave for Naval Air Station Cecil Field. With my wife in tow we had departed for Jacksonville very early in the morning as we weren't set to arrive very late at night. Finally arriving at my destination after getting lost at least twice, and after finally checking in we were able to drive to the hotel. Once we were finally able to get to sleep, but it seemed to pass by very quickly because I had to get up early for my first day of work at my new command since me and my wife were staying at a Holiday Inn while we looked around. Having checked in Aviation Intermediate

Maintenance Department I was sent to work in corrosion control where I learned how to remove and treat corrosion from aircraft avionics, aircraft parts and test equipment.

I was taught how to paint the aircraft parts, and various test equipment cases. My supervisor let me got off early from work that way I could find an apartment. Now we could move into as soon as we could. I finally found an apartment that we were able to move into and able to start unpacking are belongings that we had brought with us. Over the weekend I was able to find a living room set that I put on layaway for a little while till I was finally able to pay it off before I finally had it delivered after we had moved in. We were later able to receive the rest of our household goods, and the car that my dad had given to us. The car had been reworked by my wife's brother.

It was only a few short months after I had gotten the car that the motor blown up, and it had caught fire. I had to put that out before I went on to work. I still made it on time for work, but I still had to find a ride to, and from work till I could find another car to drive to work. One day while I was getting new tires for the car I had overheard the one of the mechanics had a car for sale. I was in need of a car because the 1973 Ford Pintos motor had blown up and caught fire. It was a car that my dad had given to me. I was able to put the fire with little damage to the car. I was still able to make it to work on time even though all that happened to me. I walked down to the Firestone tire shop to talk to him. I did find out how much he wanted for the car, and with this information in hand I went to the credit union for a personal loan to buy the car. With money in hand, I was able to buy myself an orange 1973 Chevy nova hatchback. I loved the car but it later had it challenges that started to cost me lots more money for a tune-up and to have the transmission rebuilt.

While the battleship was being towed to the gulf coast it was damaged, and had to have its bow replaced from a ship that had never been commissioned. Once the bow was replaced it continued on its journey to the gulf coast. It would never see active duty because they had started returning the battleships to the mothball fleet after the turret explosion that killed two people. It was said that it was also too expensive to maintain them. USS Coral Sea had just gotten out of dry dock after going through an extensive overhaul, when it ran into a ship collapsing its bow while it was doing night time FCLP's. It was repaired and returned to service after its repairs.

Money that I could not afford with all the other bills that I had, and it ended up sinking me farther into debt to where I had to take on a second job working at McDonald. I ended up closing the door on the end of my finger in the car door splitting finger nail open as I broke the tip and have to wear a splint on it for several weeks. I had done this while my wife was off with her family because her grandma had passed away. The following day after I had gotten injured I saw my next door neighbor outside. We stood there and talked, and he said to me that he would have taken me to the hospital if I would have just asked him.

I had wanted it, and after I had applied for the Enlisted Aviation Warfare Specialist program. Now finally having got into the program I worked hard to get my enlisted aviation warfare specialist. I had finally received it, and I now had to wait for the pinning ceremony. One day at work before my special day had arrived; I had approached my supervisor to ask him if he would like to pin my Enlisted Aviation Warfare Specialist on me. Now after the pinning ceremony was finished, my supervisor told me that it was his honor to do it for me. Mid-fall upon us so while I was at work that day my supervisor informed me was throwing a party for the shop so I took my wife to the party. I had gotten transferred to a new shop where I was working on generators, actuators and other aircraft equipment that was used on the aircraft.

Till later I ended up trading the car off for a car that was probably worse than the other car. I had ended up having the transmission rebuilt in this car as well. The nickel and dimming continued, and the struggling to keep my head above water with all the bills. To me this other car I had gotten to me was worse than the other car I traded it for and I could not wait to trade it off for another car. I had later finally traded it off for a 1991 Pontiac grand am in place of the car.

Around this time I was invited and I had taken my wife with me to a party that McDonald's was having for the crew. Also to take a break from my struggles I used to BBQ ribs, hamburgers and hot dogs after I had gotten off of work. One of the things the wife and mother-in-law wanted to do was go see the zoo. I had discovered how to get there because I had got lost on my way somewhere else. I had also heard there was a renaissance fair to be held at the zoo that weekend, and I could kill two birds at the same time. I always enjoyed that period of time and wanted to see it and learn more about it. While I was there I tried my hand at throwing than axe at a target, but I didn't do very good at it though. I just couldn't get the technique down to throw the axe properly.

I had talked to the Aviation Electrician detailer about a set of orders. Now after having thought it over, I had then decided to go to Virginia even though I would have rather stayed in Florida. I had taken house hunting leave to look for a place to live in Virginia Beach, VA where I had found a townhouse to buy but later was denied for the loan. Shortly after I had returned to work from my trip to Virginia I was approached by a chief that had worked in an office upstairs that worked with manpower. He asked if I would love to stay here if it was possible cause some was about to lose the orders cause of an injury. He later returned and informed me that my orders had been modified so I could stay in Florida for my sea duty. I was also informed to have my bags packed cause the ship was about to pull shortly.

Transfer to Sea-Op-Det, NAS Cecil Field, Florida

~ § ~

My First Cruise Over Seas

Having heard that I needed to grab my bags, and that I had to could catch the ship because it was heading out for six week rough tray. I also had in the back of my mind all of the ghost stories I had heard prior to me being transferred to NAS Cecil Field. I had thought about those ghost stories about the ship that I was to be stationed here soon, and I had wondered if the ghost that I had heard were true. These stories came from a person who had been stationed on the ship as a member of the crew. I caught a ride with a co-worker to the ship, but as I got on board I found out from the chief on watch in AIMD that the date had been pushed back a couple of months. I had to call the wife to come, and get me but I had to wait for what seemed like several hours. The weekend had passed, and it was time to get back to work at the base, while I waited for transfer to my new command. I had to wait to catch the ship as it was to pull out for rough tray in a month.

The people in my shop gave me a crash training and learning on how to run and operate the F/A-18 generator, while I waited to be deployed to the aircraft carrier. Still having my bags packed from before, and finally the time had arrived for me to depart for the *USS Forrestal (CV-59).* Most all the ships had a nick name and the Forrestal was no different. Most all the people crew referred to the ship as the Forest Fire it was called that after the big fire in the Gulf on Tonka which if of the coast of Vietnam. Working nights while I was on the ship as I ran generators, while I was deployed for six weeks. It was such a struggle to sleep I those racks during my off hours, because they were not the most comfortable things to relax in.

While I was there I had to also teach a few other shipmates how to run, fix and test the generators as inspected. The nights felt like they rolled by till we were able to pull into port to pick up guest of the shipmates, and now that everyone was abroad we set sail again for the day. Now that we were far enough out to sea, and now we were able to launch aircraft for an air show for the guest and the crew. Now with the planes airborne the captain came over the 1MC calling everyone to the flight deck to view the air show.

There was an F-14 Tomcat that made one pass as it lined up for a second pass, and during that pass it broke the sound barrier. The plane rocked the ship from the sound wave it generated with its sound breaking pass. Once the air show over and the planes back on board we set sail back to port to let of the guest, and some members of the crew were able to visit family for the night. The night passed by quickly as caught a ride back the ship. We could get underway early that morning. Once back on board I went to my berthing area and went back to sleep. That way I could be ready to work the night shift. Once now at sea we had spent another three weeks performing flight operations and drills needed for the upcoming cruise. The days seem to run together as we ran generator after generator until it was time to pull back into port. Once back in port we departed back to our home base at Naval Air Station Cecil Field.

It was after a couple days off then it was back to work in the generator shop until it was time for the cruise. It is nice to only work 5 days and have the weekends off, cause soon that will come to an end when I am back aboard ship again for the cruise. The day came for me to depart on cruise on board the *USS Forrestal (CV-59.* Once aboard the ship and settled into my rack and then chilled out in the berthing for the rest of the day. Seven AM came early the following morning, and after muster I was able to return to my rack to rest until I had to get up prior to my shift that evening. My alarm goes off long before most people were starting to stir. Grabbing a quick shower before I had to get dressed and eat before I needed to be at work.

I got up early enough but had to wait in some long lines. I had to figure out which galley I would like to eat in. Finally getting my food I quickly eat it as wait in a line to put my dirty tray and silverware. Now I get back to the berthing to hang out for a little while before my 12 hour shift to start at 7 PM. Sitting and listening as we got a pass down from the day check before the supervisor went to the maintenance meeting. Now sitting there as we wait until the supervisor to come back to pass out what maintenance has for us to do for the night. Finally getting our plan put together part of go work on batteries in the battery shop as the rest of us mount a generator on the bench for training all night as we float around off the coast as we waited around for our planes to come aboard. Finally with all our planes aboard the ship starts to conduct flight ops as they float around off the coast conducting squadron carrier qualifications for all their pilots.

Now with the air wing carrier qualifications finished the ship set sail for the Mediterranean Sea. They continued flight operations as they crossed the Atlantic Ocean. We were at sea few days before we finally passed the Straits of Gibraltar, before we entered into the Mediterranean Sea. We head to relieve the *USS Theodore Roosevelt (CVN-71)* on station. Finally after relieving the ship we sailed to our operating sector of the Mediterranean Sea as we began patrolling the no fly zones with our planes in Iraq. Finally after we floated around in circles as we flew sorties over Iraq for several weeks. We had a briefing about the do and don'ts before we pulled in to Israel for our first port of call. We were told not to leave any bags our back packs unattended cause they would be picked up a disposed of by the Israel police. Once in port and liberty was called each I changed my cloths and jumped in line to ether catch a ferry or a ships boat that they used to carry sailors to the beach.

Once we finally reached the beach, and off loaded the ferry. We could still smell the salt water in the air. We caught the bus on the pier to the USO in Haifa, Israel, and from there we wondered around the city and the mall that was up on a hill. The hill gave us a view of the ship anchored out in the harbor. While wondering around the city we found a local place to eat, while we were wondering about the city sightseeing. It was now late in the evening, and I caught the bus back to the landing. To catch the ferry back to the *USS Forrestal (CV-59)*, while the windblown salt water waves hit you in the face. We were finally able to get on the ferry after we had to wait in a long line with fellow shipmates.

Once loaded, we were pushed away from the pier and set out for the ship. I had finally reached the ship, and once off the ferry. The salt from the salt water spray that had hit me on the ferry ride to and from the ship, and the smell of salt was still in the air, and on my face, arms and clothes as I walked back to the berthing. I hung out in the lounge and watched a little television with the person that was on berthing watch. Time had come for me to grab a shower and get some sleep. My duty day started at 7 AM. I had to get up early for muster and then have to stand my watch before I could get a shower and go back to bed. Morning came early, and after muster I could change my clothes. Then I could get off the ship and spend the day in town.

Now off the ship after I had taken the ferry to the pier to catch a bus ride up the hill to the USO where I got something to eat, and hang out till I was ready to go back to the ship. While in the city, I got to wonder around looking at the different sites as we could look out over the waters, and the ship anchored as we stood there on the hill. Now after having spent a few days in port, the ship finally weighed anchor and headed back to the ships assigned operating area. Shortly thereafter we was underway man overboard was called away, and we had to get up out of are racks and go to are shops to be mustered and hang out for a bit until are supervisor said we could go back to the berthing and sleep. Once finally in range the ship began flying sorties in support of the no fly zones.

Now after a few days at sea we got to pull into Rhodes, Greece. The ship anchored out in the harbor, and now we had to catch a ferry to carry us into the port. Once in port I walk into town passing through a gate in the medi-eval city wall. Once past the city wall you get a good sense of islands medi-eval past. I wondered around the city looking at the different shops and the pubs with in the city walls. Once walking outside of the city wall you see the beaches, a more modern looking part of the town.

Walking around the beach you could see a medieval fort that over looked the inlet of the bay and lots tourists and town's people laying out on the beach and enjoying the sun. It was after several fun days there. That we pulled back out to sea once more. The same old routine started up once again now that we were back floating around.

We had pulled back into Rhodes, Greece, and then on to Haifa, Israel, Alexandria, Egypt, and Souda Bay, Crete. It was while I was in Marseille, France that I took a tour, where I got to see a medieval castle, and several medieval churches. I also remember to myself at how this was a place that possibly where my ancient ancestors had walked long ago. I had gotten really interested in where they had come from. Then it was on to Palma, Spain, Toulon, France, and Antalya, Turkey. We pulled back out to sea to await the relief of the *USS America (CV-66)*.

Once now that the ship was finally replaced we set sail through the Straits of Gibraltar and out into the Atlantic Ocean as we were now on are way home. Finally on our way home we hit Bermuda Island to on load reservists and tigers as we let some of the crew fly home early while the rest sail on to our home port. Home finally we had to wait till everything was set up to disembark the ship. Once able to get off the ship and boarding awaiting buses to take us back to the base. A well-deserved few days off with the wife, before I had to go back to work on the base. It does seem like life has passed you by once you have gotten back home, because it seems like there is so much to catch up on that you had missed out on.

The cruise made me feel like my Viking ancestors, and I traveled in same waters my Viking ancestors had sailed in over 1000 years earlier. That was a special feeling to have traveled in the same footsteps they did.

My Navy Duties Post cruise

It was very nice to have a few days off after being gone for many months out to sea. I had spent those days off having a good time with my wife and friends. Now getting back to work, I had impressed all with my newfound skills, and they were impressed because I had never been able to run the generators by myself. I was off and running, troubleshooting and quality-checking one generator after another. It seemed like the work would never end, and I was able to take a break. I got all the information that Diane had gathered about the family while on my family vacation. I now had all the information in hand, and after I returned home from vacation. I went to work on research on my family. I tried to do as much as I could in between my duties with the military. I had to take a break while on cruise too, but I always picked it up again later.

On the *USS George Washington (CVN-73)*

There was soon talk I would be sent to the *USS George Washington (CVN-73)* for its shakedown cruise. It had just completed its commissioning and trials before we came onboard for the cruise that was to last six weeks. It was my job to run nights to help in the standing up of the generator shop as it had just come out of the dry dock. I was charged with locating and identifying the test equipment the shop would need to test all of the generators they were going to test and troubleshoot during the cruise, while we were running and troubleshooting generators and aircraft batteries.

The work between all of the drills continued as we operate all of the aircraft generators and batteries that came into the shop while we were in the Bahaman waters for several weeks. It was nice to finally, after those long weeks and days, to be pulling into Fort Lauderdale for a few days of fun and rest. One day while walking into the city, we walked by this high-end car dealership that dealt in cars such as Porsche, Lotus, Jaguar, Ferrari, and Lamborghini. It was nice to look at the cars and dream about owning one as we continued our walk into the city.

I got to see from the ship many of the local and tourist enjoying a day on the water in the yachts, and how much of a tease they can be. Now after our days of rest, we went back to sea to sea for a few more weeks of flying and ships drills. The last few days, we were called together as a department where we were given a certificate signifying that we were a plank owner on the *USS George Washington (CVN-73)*. Finally, we pulled back into Norfolk, Virginia, and in an orderly manner we off-loaded the ship. Once the ship was off-loaded in Norfolk, Virginia the squadrons and the Sea-Op-Det detachment, flew back to our home base in Jacksonville, Florida.

Back at NAS Cecil Field

After a few days off, I was soon back at work on the base, running, troubleshooting, and performing collateral duty inspections on aircraft generators as they came through the door. The Sea-Op-Det personnel shuffle was on since the person who was in the detachment with the *USS America (CV-66)* was getting out soon and me being next in line that meant I would be taking his place soon. He was also filling me in on what the *USS America (CV-66)* was like. I continued to do my work in the shop and also spent time with my wife while awaiting the Med. cruise. It was a handful of people who started working night check in the generator shop until I was set to go out on the ship.

I did make good use of my time that I had at home before I had to go to the ship. The day for me to depart for Norfolk, Virginia, came, and they dropped me off at the air terminal to catch an air lift, I had to catch a flight to the ship that was departing the following day. While I was doing research on the family, I found out that Great-grandfather Ole P. was a carpenter and his father Ole K. was a journeymen blacksmith. I thought this was interesting because I had liked working with a forge in my ag. shop class. I enjoyed creating different things, like a branding iron and then cutting holes in heated metal rod before I cut it in half. I made some different metal chisels. This is part of what I would have imagined Ole K., Great-Great Grandfather, would have been for him.

Ole K. had settled in and now was ready to start his apprenticeship with the resident journeyman blacksmith in Hakadal, Norway. Ole discussed his training with Hans, and he told Ole that he would start off by stoking the fire

of the forage, while Ole watched Hans work. Ole would have to carry the coal for the fire, and he would have to be patient for he would get his chance. Hans, while Ole helped twist the pieces of metal together and once the twisting the yellow hot metal

together. They started the process of hammering out a sword. Hans shifted the coals around while poking the metal that would become a sword into the fire. Ole bellowed the fire for the forage making the coals grow hotter around the metal.

Hans from the forage pulled out the yellow hot metal with a set of tongs. He quickly placed the hot metal on the anvil. The hammer striking the yellow hot piece metal with a loud clang causing sparks. Brief sparks from the shifting of the coals in the forage while the metal poked into the forage. Ole bellowed the fire while watching Hans work the yellow hot metal he pulled out of the hot coals. Quickly placing the yellow hot metal on to the anvil, and with a mighty below the smith's hammer, with a clang, hit the hot metal. Each swing of Hans's hammer hit the metal before returning it to the forage fire. Shifting the coals of the fire causing sparks while the metal is shifted around in the fire.

Hans pulling the yellow hot metal out of the fire before placing it over the anvil, and hitting it with a mighty clang of the hammer hitting the metal. He had finished the sword, the blade still needed tempered and honed. There was still a process the blade had to go through before it could be tempered and honed. Hans explained the sword first needed to be annealed, which is the hardening of the metal. Hans placed the sword into the fire till it was cherry red. Once hot enough he pulled it from the fire, and buried the blade under the ground for 24 hours.

Once that process was complete, Hans sent Ole out for a bucket of water. The sword being un-buried and returned to the forage fire till it was yellow hot. Hans returned with the water, and once the sword was hot enough. Hans instructed Ole on how to finish making the sword. Hans let Ole remove the sword from the fire. That way he could watch the sword tip reach a purple color, and then plunged into the bucket of water sizzling from the hot blade in the water. Thus tempering and hardening the blade and now ready for the honing process of the blade.

I found out he was also a cottager, and continued my search for other facts about my family.

My Cruise on the *USS America (CV-66)*

Finally in Norfolk, Virginia, I got to settle into my berthing to get ready for the ship's departure. I was the supervisor of the day shift in the generator shop, but it was still combined with the rest of shops in 620, where aviation electricians worked. I did learn something about the rest of work center 620 besides the rest of my duties I had to do on the ship. We were underway now as we played around for a few days, so that the planes could complete their carrier qualifications before the ship departed for its Mediterranean cruise. Now with complete carrier qualifications, we turned tail and departed the Atlantic Ocean for the Mediterranean Sea. We passed through the Strait of Gibraltar and into the Mediterranean Sea to relieve the *USS Theodore Roosevelt (CVN-71)*.

Now, with the *USS Theodore Roosevelt (CVN-71)* relieved, we were now underway for the next six months. Once the turnover was complete, the ship sailed through the Ionian Sea and into the Adriatic Sea, where they were to operate from. We floated around, as the planes flew, in support of operations over Bosnia and Herzegovina, Croatia, and Serbia. The leader of Germany visited that was known as the Balkans. A plot was hatched to assassinate the German leader which started World War 1. These countries after World War II made up the former Yugoslavia nation which was part of the eastern bloc during the cold war with Russia. This area is a hot bed of war and conflict, and this area has sparked many wars and conflicts.

The *USS America (CV-66)* started its operations before its first port of call in Trieste, Italy. Once in port, we were finally able to get off the boat by rank, but we wait for our rank to be finally called away over the 1mc. Now once it was called away we had to stand in long lines to finally disembark the ship. Once on the ferry, I decided to sit up top, and I was able to see the ferry pull away from the ship. You could feel the seawater hit you in the face as the ferry pitched up and down over the water. Once beside the camel, we had to watch or step as we disembarked the ferry. Now finally on land, the first thing I did was to find a currency exchange place. This way I would have local currency to spend in the shops and on food and drinks.

I and my partner walked around some of the cobble streets for a while, looking at the different shops the city, and then we tried to find a place to eat and get something to drink. Some of their streets are still cobble stones but not all of them though. The ferry rides at night, if you rode up top, could get chilly from the wind. We got to make the most of our time on shore before we had to return to the ship and return to the sea. Once the ship had weighed anchor and was back out to sea. The ship resumed its normal routine and flight operations.

It was on to Corfu, Greece, after we had spent a few weeks out to sea. Now, once we were in port, it was time to get of the ship, but we had to wait in longs to finally get off the ship. Once off the ship it was time to exchange US money for the local currency and then it was on to finding where to get some good food. It was always nice to eat something else other than boat food. We did get to look around some of the local, even though it was cool and rained outside, but there was still a good to be had had in port in spite of the elements.

The fun was soon over, and we were back at sea now, resuming the normal ship routine as flight operations went on at a busy pace. Work continued as I counted down the days until we pulled into port. The day was finally here when we pulled into Trieste, Italy. We were finally able to get off the ship after waiting our turn in the long lines. The time came as I exchanged money and had to find some where to eat. The city had a lot to offer, so we walked around after eating. I and a few others from the ship took a tour of Slovenia, where we saw an underground cave and Predjama Castle that was built into the side of a mountain.

The Predjama Castle had chambers and tunnels that extend the length of the mountain, but those tunnels had been sealed to the public. It was nice to have the time off of the ship before we had to head back to sea once more, but finally that day arrived, and we were back at sea again. Now with the ship back on its station, word got around that the next few port calls were canceled and that we had new orders to transit through the Suez Canal and relieve the *USS Abraham Lincoln (CVN-72)*, and that way it could continue on with it cruise.

The *USS America (CV-66)* now turned and headed south through the Suez Canal, Gulf of Suez, Red Sea and through the Gulf of Aden, and we could see the shore and some houses in Egypt as we transited through the ditch. The ship was now on station off the coast of Somalia after we completed the transit. Now the ship was there to support ongoing operations in Somalia after they had relieved the *USS Abraham Lincoln*

(CVN-72). It was hot and humid floating around in the Indian Ocean, and it did make it tough there.

We still continue normal operations and flight ops on the ship. The ship did get the opportunity to drop below the equator and conduct an ancient ceremony of the mariners for crossing the line. This is a rite that had evolved from Viking rituals, executed upon crossing the thirtieth parallel, that is passed down from mariner to mariner. King Neptune sent Davey Jones and his entourage to visit the ship the night before the ceremony. The day had arrived for the shell backs to wake the pollywogs and take them through the ceremony and to meet King Neptune who had arrived that morning to sit over the crossing the line ceremony.

Once finally relieved, the ship steamed north as it transited through the Gulf of Aden, where it conducted flight operations in the Red Sea on its way through Gulf of Suez and Suez Canal as we made port in Haifa, Israel. We got off the ship after liberty has been secured for rough seas. Once the seas had settled, we were now able to get off the ship for a little rest and relaxation, which was well earned after being at sea for a number of days.

You could feel the motion of the ferry as it cuts through the water. Once on land I went on a bus ride with my buddy to the mall, where we looked around the different shops there. While in Israel you never want to leave your bag unattended because it would not be there once you returned. Israelis take their security serious and would do away with unattended bags because of that. Soon, we were back to sea as we continued north to the Ionian Sea and taking up station in the Adriatic Sea.

We floated around for a while before making a port of call in Marseille, France. We had to wait in line to catch a ferry or a motor whale boat once we were onboard able to pull away from the ship, and head into port. I got to see the city and take a tour of a medieval castle that had its own church and dungeon and its own escape tunnel. We could see different French-made weapons hanging on the walls in this one room that they could use to escape into the countryside. We also got to see lots of the countryside, church, grape vineyard, and ruins of a castle and church.

Now back at sea for a while it was on to our next port visit in Palma, Spain. Once in port and after a ferry ride to the beach, it was to change money and then on to get something to eat.

The place was Texas Jack where we enjoyed a bowl of and a beer. Now it was on to explore the city and the shops and even this area where they had some underground shops that wasn't well-lit, and we only went there during the day. Once the ship was back to sea it was on to Malaga, Spain, and soon home. The ship was finally relieved by the *USS George Washington (CVN-73)*. Once relieved, the *USS America (CV-66)* made transit through the Straits of Gibraltar. Now that the ship was through straits, it made a transit across the Atlantic Ocean for its home port in Norfolk, Virginia. Now safe in port, we were able to get off the ship and catch a transport for home in Florida.

Our Home Port

We set foot back at NAS Cecil Field after our flight home. We did get a few days off before we had to come back to work on the base. Once back at the shop, I was able to return to my normal duties there. Finally a sense of normal has returned now once back at home and away from the ship. I and one other guy from the shop got sent to Norfolk, Virginia, for a weekend detachment onboard the *USS John F. Kennedy (CV-67)* to test out the generator bench and to certify the bench. Once done, I had to make arrangements for the return trip home. One of the changes I liked was that we got to work out three days a week while at work.

Things were changing around AIMD and the generator shop. The shop was to get its first woman to work in the shop. We went to lunch together, and got lunch for the other people that we worked with. We also worked out together three times a week. Liz and I became the best of friends. I got sent to Norfolk, Virginia, on a detachment for a couple weeks onboard the *USS Theodore Roosevelt (CVN-71)* to work in the generator shop, and once home, I returned to my normal routine.

I invited Liz and another friend over for cook outs after work at the apartment. We got to see a movie together as a shop. I also got to spend time at their house for BBQ as well as my apartment. Soon I was up for orders, so I need to talk to my detailer about a new set of orders. I had a sneaky feeling with some signs at home, and that was confirmed by a visit to the clinic on the base. Della and I found out that she was pregnant. The first person I told, after we had found out the results of the test, was my friend Liz.

It was after I had told Liz that we were off for a cross-country trip to the west coast. The first stop on our cross-country trip was to see my sister Marilyn in Lake Charles, Louisiana where we spent a few days visiting with my sister. While we were at my sister's, we got to see the carnival and enjoy some great local food. I also got to spend some time with my older brother Charles who lived there, and I hadn't seen him since I was a little kid. During that visit my sister did tell me about their life there which was a 180 degree different form my life. I can say I understand what she told but I really don't because I didn't live the life that they lived.

I got to live a lot of what that part of my family was robbed of, but I was also robbed of a life that I could have had with my brothers and sisters growing up. My parents and brothers and sister were the true victims of a true vindictive ex-husband did to them. We was on the freeway in Texas when we got passed by cars in the fast line looking out the passenger window I seen a pick-up passing on the right side. We got to Wichita Falls, Texas where we decided to spend the night. No sooner then we got there the signs of a storm coming and we could see the people that lived scrabbling to leave and head for shelter.

We did hurry up and ate fast and headed to find a motel room. Just as we found a place to stay the rain and hail hit the place. We laid there and listened and watched it storm out from our motel room. We went on to see my sister Diane and her husband and their kids in Colorado Springs, Colorado. We were able to spend some good quality time together visiting each other. It was soon that we went on to make a visit in Las Vegas, Nevada, and stay at the Excalibur.

We got to see the dinner show and were supposed to meet her parents there, but they had backed out. We had spent a day there, and it was on to home as we stayed in Provo, Utah. I never did find the cemetery while I was in Provo which had nice since Great Grand-pa and Great Grand-ma was buried there. It was a nice stay at home in Idaho before we headed out for Lemoore, California, where I was to be stationed. The whole trip could have been better planned out, so that I didn't not have to do some back tracking which made the journey even longer,

Transfer to California and VFA-137

~ § ~

NAMTRA

Once I had reported into the base, it was off to find an apartment to stay in while I was stationed here. I was to report to NAMTRA for technical training before I had to report for my final duty station at VFA-137. I arrived in town early, and was able to look around the city and get settled in before I had to start my class. I had also gotten my wife into the navy hospital for regular pregnancy checkups. We had been assigned to a midwife who was of Swedish descent. I also went with my wife to all of her regular checkups. I really did enjoy the level of care and interaction we had with the midwife.

I had just started my training at NAMTRA before going to my ultimate duty station. I had to study the books and take the tests. As a class, we also got some on the hands training on the F/A-18. It was some long nights of studying and training with the technical manuals. I passed my class, and got transfer early to VFA-137 because I had taken cable and wire bundle repair before I had left NAS Cecil Field.

Stationed at VFA-137

I have finally reached my ultimate duty station on the west coast. Now, my hands-on aircraft training was to really start with the rest of the aviation electrician shop. I still continued to make the checkups with my wife to see how our first child was doing. I had gotten to the shop just in time to make my first detachment aboard the *USS Constellation (CV-64)*. The first few days of the detachment were spent conducting carrier qualifications and then on to the rest of the training after the carrier qualifications were complete.

We made a port call in San Francisco, California, and I got to take in a few of the sights there before we were back at sea. Now, back at sea, I continued to work on my shop qualifications and my final checker qualifications while we were stationed on the ship. It was worth more to work on it onboard the ship. The ship picked up where it had left off and continued transit for Vancouver, British Columbia, Canada. While on our transit to Vancouver, I got to see several whales swimming off the coast of Washington and Canada.

I got to take a look around the city after eating and exchanging some money. I and some friends took a walk through the park and around the bay. The path led us up to the Vancouver Bridge, back to the park, and back to town. I made my way back the ship, and the following day I got to spend some time in gas town. We had gotten there early, and having gotten there early, we decided to eat and have a drink at this Irish pub within sight of the steam clock. Gas town is where I got to see and hear a unique clock that was powered by steam. I had also enjoyed eating out after eating boat food for some days. Once back at to sea it was back to the same routine as we made the transit for home.

The day was getting there as we broke down the shops for the transit back to our home. It was soon that we would be reunited with our loved ones as well. It was after a few months I was transferred to night shift. I could really learn how to work on the F/A-18. It was on night check where most of all the work is done. That night check could get the planes up for the next day of flight operations. There were some very long nights spent working on the planes till we finally got to go home for the night and with a little kid at home it made it even more of a challenge.

We had made other workup detachments to San Diego, California, and the ship made port of calls in San Francisco, California. I had walked around a lot of the city, but I was always aware of what was going on around me. A person I went out in town with had his white hat stolen off his head by a person who was riding on a bicycle. It all happened really fast that night, but I could see he was up to something. We had made a detachment in Roswell, New Mexico. While we were there we got hit by a sandstorm almost every night. Rick, His brother-in-law and me after would change are clothes and catch the bus that would take us out into town.

One of trips out in town would find us caught in a sand storm while we tried to make are way to the mall. Luckily a commuter bus came to are rescue and allowed us to take shelter from the sand storm in the bus. One of our favorite places to eat was the Dutch Kitchen. We had to make several detachments to the Naval Air Station Fallon in Fallon, Nevada, and I did get to gamble a little while I was there. It was one that I was able to stay back from a detachment that I was able to go with to her appointment.

It was during the checkup that we discussed the baby's due date, and it was within days. It was with the test that they had run that they found out she needed to have a C-section. It was with that that a new boy was brought into the world. We named the new baby Lars, and he was born on December 8, 1995. I got to spend a few weeks at home with Lars, but soon it was back to work. It was some long and hard work till the day drew very near and the day we had to break down the entire shop. Once the shop was broken down and packed up, it was time for us to pack up and catch a transport to San Diego, California, where we could store our gear away and set up our shops for the cruise. I had to catch a bus for a detachment to MATTC Miramar base while the ship is underway. The detachment at MATTC Miramar was there to catch planes that were flying back forth while the ship was conducting carrier qualifications.

It was next morning that we had to catch a C-2 transport to make a carrier landing on board the ship. Once our small detachment was on board the ship, and the *USS Constellation (CV-64)* could continue on its transit across the Pacific Ocean. The ship conducted flight ops as it made its transit toward our first port of call. The day we pulled pier side in Sydney, Australia came, and we were able to get off the ship for a well-needed rest. I and some other people got off the ship and able to look around the city after we exchanged money to got some food at the local restaurant. We got to look around the city and the casino before we had to pull back out to sea. Now once back at sea, the ship made time for our next port of call. The ship, after a few days at sea, now pulled pier side in Fremantle, Australia. Now pier side, it was only a matter of waiting in long lines before we were able to get off of the ship.

Finally, once off the ship, the group I was with head to town to exchange some money and to find something to eat as well. The place we had chosen to eat at was right on the beach and had a wonderful view of the surf and the ocean. We sat there and ate, talked, and watched the surf roll in on the beach. We all tried to figure out what we were going to do after we were done eating, so we headed for town to look around some of the local shops.

One of the places in town we had found was a place that made their own waffle cones as we had to get an ice cream cone from the shop. We got together as a group and walked off the ship and headed to the train station because we were going to head for Perth and some other towns in between, where we got to enjoy the heights of the country side and the sights the city had to offer. I did get to look around Arthur's head and the round house as it overlooked the ocean. It was soon that the ship was back at sea and headed for the rest of the cruise.

The ships transit around Australia through the Indian Ocean headed north. We had crossed the equator and at the 180th meridian (International Date Line), and we had met qualifications to qualify to be a golden shellback. It was on the ship's transit that we got a visit from Davey Jones as they were about to cross the equator during the night. Me being a shellback, I helped to round up the pollywogs and take them to their breakfast and through the initiation. Now, once that was over and cleaned up, the ship returned to its normal routine.

We continued it trek north through the Arabian Sea, Gulf of Oman, Strait of Hormuz, and into the Persian Gulf. The *USS Constellation (CV-64)* and its air wing was there to enforce UN sanctions and patrol the no-fly zones over Iraq. The ship had made port of calls in and out of Jabal Ali, while we got to explore the city of Dubai. I and a few other friends made the most of or time there in port. We got to enjoy the local entertainment and food after we had exchanged some of money for the local currency. This was in between the ship conducting its normal routine and operations in the Gulf.

A Day on the *USS Constellation (CV-64)*

I was just done with breakfast, so I went back to the berthing before I went to the shop. I gathered my stuff and went up to the shop. I checked in with the supervisor when I arrived for the start of my twelve-hour shift onboard the ship. The supervisor got the pass down from the night check supervisor before he went to the maintenance meeting, so I sat there and waited for him to return from the meeting. Finally, the supervisor returned, and he gave me the notes from the meeting, while I waited for the morning flight ops to begin. Soon the phone rang, and it was from my friend in the troubleshooters shack. He was looking to see if I wanted to do the final check on the planes. Of course I said yes, I told my supervisor and grabbed my flight deck gear and headed to the troubleshooters shack. As a group, we walked from the shop to the flight deck to find the planes that were listed on the flight schedule.

Once we located the planes, we began the preflight checks on the planes. I talked to the plane captain, the flight deck coordinator, and the flight deck quality assurance as we waited for the flight operations to begin. I checked over the plane while I waited for the pilot to arrive. Once the pilot arrives, he talks to the plane captain and the troubleshooters. The plane captain follows the pilot up the ladder to assist him in buckling in the seat of the plane. I stood there and waited while the pilot went through his preflight checks. It was just then air boss came over the 5mc, telling the pilots to startup of the engines on the go aircraft. The plane captain guides the pilot through the start-up of the engines and the preflight checks, and I stood there and observed the movements of the aircraft surfaces. Soon, the plane director comes over and took control of the aircraft, calling for the chains to be broken down as he moves the plane into line to be launched off the aircraft carrier.

I followed the aircraft to the shot line, where I stood and watched the other aircraft launched as we waited on our aircraft to arrive to the catapult. I crouched down below the flight deck while the aviation ordinance men arm the aircraft. Then we moved into position to check the aircraft. The aircraft is moved into position. We check the plane over to make sure it's ready for launch. Once I have checked it over, I moved into position, so I can see all of the movements, surfaces, and see the planes lights if the come on. I crouch down into position and watch the plane director move the aircraft into the shuttle to be launched.

The catapult technician crawled along, while the plane director moved the plane into the hold back position, as he brings the plane to military power. The plane goes through its final movements, we give thumbs up, and the shooter shoots the plane off the deck. I move across to the other side and meet up with my partner. We high-five each other before we go to meet up with the rest of the crew to see if we can help them out. Then we all go down to the shop together once our planes were off the deck. Now we talk to each other and wait for the next launch and the recovery of the airborne aircraft.

The shop had changed faces several times during the cruise as they departed the ship to begin a new chapter of their life. I had made a mistake and got in trouble for that mistake and could not final check the planes on the deck after that. It was that made the cruise a little more enjoyable, but the change in supervisors was made within the shop for me to go to day shift. I still made the most of my time on the ship, and learned all I could learn on the plane.

The Transit Out of the Zone

The ship's high tempo operations gulf were soon widening down as we prepared for the transit out of the Gulf, and once are transit was complete, the ship began to conduct normal ships training and flight operations. During the ship's transit, we got to enjoy ports of calls in Singapore, where I got to see the Merlion and some of the malls. It was during the visit in Singapore that I got to take a tour of Malaysia and see how their handmade textiles were made. We made a transit to Hong Kong, and we were the first United States ship to visit right after the British turned it back over to China.

The fun part of the visit was to see the city's night line light up at night as we rode the ferry back to the ship. Then we made a transit on to Sasebo, Japan, and then on to pick up the tigers in Everett, WA. I got to fly home early on the advance detachment from Washington to help get things set up for the main body's return home after their stay at sea. It was during the cruise that I had extended my stay with the squadron, and that way I could complete the cruise with them. I had also been in contact with my detailer about new orders to my next duty station. It was during my time at home that I found out what happened while I was away at sea.

It so happened that I was on watch at the time that I got a call from a debt collector, and with some other digging, I was able to uncover the gravity of the financial disaster that my wife had created for me to deal with now that I was back home. Now I was faced with two decisions, and one was work with a debt counselor or just goes ahead and declares bankruptcy. But I wanted to avoid doing just that. I had also gotten my orders to my new duty station and had taken some time off in transit to my new duty station.

I was now forced into bankruptcy, and I had to deal with that while I was on leave. It was during this that I had lost all trust in her to deal with and handle the finances. Now I could take control over the finances once more, and clean up the financial mess she created for me. Unfortunately I was forced to file bankruptcy cause of the mess. I left the family behind and returned to California and checked into my new duty station. I look at my little boy once I got home, and I can see how much I had missed out on while I was gone out on the cruise. It does make you appreciate the time you do get spend at home with the family and friends.

Transfer to VFA-125

I had checked in and gotten a room in the barracks, while I had to wait for on-base housing. I got to work in my new shop, where my training and learning had begun on the different jets that the squadron owned. There were lots to learn about all those different jets that they had in the squadron. I had gotten chosen for an up and coming detachment that was in El Centro, California. I was there in support of a training detachment they were making to the base. I did get to enjoy some of the things that base had to offer on my off time, but soon it was time for us to depart and return to our home base in Lemoore, California. I was sent to the corrosion shop with the squadron now that I have on-base housing. I now moved my family back to California, and now we are a complete family once again.

I took advantage of that time and went to West Hills College and took classes for an associate degree in business administration. I had to work very hard at balancing my time between work, family, and being able to do my studies for college. I went back to college because my time in the U.S. Navy was coming to an end soon, and I wanted to prepare myself for life after the navy. The other reason why I went to college was my work schedule. I am still working on completing college. I was also trying to find out more about where and when my ancestors had come to the United States, but the search continues one step at a time.

I found out that my wife was pregnant and now expecting our second child. We had chosen the same midwife who had delivered our first son, and now she was to see and deliver our second child. I was there for all of her checkups. It was as time went by that the baby was born on the first of September 2000, and found out it was a boy. We named this boy James after her dad. This made two boys in the family now. I had also begun to grow, explore changes in my life as time went along. I had begun to talk about to some changes with some people online. I had learned a lot from them. I learned a lot about me and what was really dear to me. I wanted to learn more about the world of business because I was looking for a change in experience. I had worked as an aviation electrician for a while, and I was looking for a change and a bigger challenge to conquer.

I enjoyed a wonderful friendship with Vicki and Denise, and Vicki told me about Shannon. It would have been nice to have talked and gotten to know Shannon earlier than I did. It was hard to communicate with them, and I was limited in the way I could communicate with them. I hated those limitations, but I had to deal with them. I did make the best I could do out of the situation. Vicki had also helped me with some ideas on what to write for my research papers that I had to do for college classes. I also wrote some of my college term papers about the Vikings and the medieval time of history. I had also enjoyed going to Renaissance fairs because I was always fascinated by the medieval period of history. I also bought my first sword from a vendor at the fair. One of the things I was really interested in was the webs that had people attached and water poured down in front of the person attached to the web.

I found a Swedish village nearby where I was stationed and the one store there was selling Scandinavian items. One day while I was shopping at the store the owner told me about a Son of Norway lodge that meets the second Friday of each in Visalia's Veterans memorial building. The second Friday of the month had arrived and I really wanted to go to the meeting and I also asked my wife if she wanted to go with me but she said no. I went on without her to the meeting and I left early because I wasn't sure how to get to the place. I did have a tough finding the place, but I did finally arrive at the place where the meeting was to be held. I introduced myself to all that was in attendance at that meeting and they invited me to come back the following month as well. I kept in mind the date of the next meeting so that I wouldn't forget to go to the meeting.

The day did arrive for the next meeting of the Son of Norway. The meeting begun with a potluck and then after we had finished eating the meeting was opened by Mr. Scrabeck the President of the lodge. The meeting begun with the singing of the Norwegian National anthem followed with a reading about the life of King Harold Hardrada. I was also given a membership form to fill out so that I could join the lodge. I did fill but then I left for my next duty station at VFA-151. I never did make it back to another meeting, but I had never forgotten about the people and the friendships I had made at the Son of Norway lodge #6-115.

Transfer to VFA-151

Time had come for me to search for new orders to a new duty station, but my choices were very narrow because I was now locked into the F-18 community. I had decided on orders to VFA-151, and I knew I would be returning to a ship that I had already known. Now with orders in hand, I check out of the squadron and went home on leave till it was time to check-in to my new duty station. It was while I was there that I made some good friends in and out of the squadron.

Stationed at VFA-151

I had now checked in with my new squadron, and quickly got to work in my new shop. We had an upcoming detachment to the *USS Constellation (CV-64)* that was home ported in San Diego, California. We were to be making a port of call in San Francisco, California, in the up and coming workup. No sooner than I had gotten back from a work-up and then than Della went through my things in my duffle bag. Now that the ship's workups were done and now the ship is away on its cruise. I was having a pretty routine port of call until I got to my first port visit in Sydney, Australia. I got off the boat and found an Internet cafe, to check my e-mail. I got that strange feeling when I got into my e-mail, and when I got to thinking about what I was seeing when I viewed my account. It wasn't an exciting way to start off my port visit in Sydney.

I was still worried and very mad, because I had a lot of personal e-mail letters and pictures in my e-mail inbox. I dealt with what I could and tried to go about enjoying the rest of the port visit before we had to return to the normal routine of the cruise. I tried not to worry about what was going on with my personal e-mail, but it was still in the back of my mind. I also tried to find out from Snowy what was going on, but I never got an answer from her. I got an e-mail from Denise's husband some time later though. His e-mail didn't make me feel all that much better as I really wasn't sure what was going on there. I enjoyed the rest of the port and now we were back to sea. Now the ship was in Fremantle, Australia for its next port visit. It was pretty much a routine port visit and soon we're back to sea and holding our crossing the line ceremony. Now that was done with the ceremony, we made our way to where the USS *Constellation* would be conducting its flight operations.

Now once on station in the Persian Gulf, and some time had passed by we were on to our next port visit in Jabal Ali, UAE. The port visit was some well-earned down time a pretty routine visit. I had been talking to Vicki, and she told me about this gal she knew. I was interested in meeting with Shannon, but I couldn't talk to her through one of the other chat means on the Internet because my wife had a jealous temper that I had to deal with. I really hadn't had much contact with Shannon other than by e-mail, but she was someone I wanted to get to know. The only other contact I had with her was through Vicki, who I had gotten to know via the Internet. It was while I was on cruise that I was told what was going on with Shannon through Vicki. I found out about that Shannon had gone into hiding because she was in a very bad and abusive relationship.

I was thousands of miles away from home when Vicki informed me about what was going on there. It is like when life passes you by when you are out on cruise, and there is so much you have to catch up on once you return home from overseas. I had decided to e-mail Shannon to let her know I was thinking of her and was praying for her safety, but that was all I could do since I was thousands of miles away from any one. I did keep Shannon in my thoughts and prayers while I was away cause of what she was going through at the time. I did keep in contact with Vicki who had contact with Shannon. I still cared about Shannon, even though we were no more than an acquaintance of her and Vicki, who kept me informed on what was happening back home. She never really knew me, and I only had known about her through Vicki other than by a few e-mails we had exchanged back and forth.

We had a few more port visits in Jabal Ali, UAE. Now the ship was able to leave behind the hot humid weather of the Persian Gulf, and make the slow trek for home. The training of the pilots and crew continued that way they could stay qualified and their skills sharp. Unfortunately an F-14 Tomcat crashed on the way home. It was an unfortunate crash after an accident cruise up to that point that seen a lot of up tempo days in the Persian Gulf.

The training was also carried out for the benefit with the other countries that are allies of the United States. Training with other countries is critical way of getting the other countries in the area to work together and it shows how well other countries can work together. Plus it is a good way to know what to expect from your partner countries if needed to work together in live situations. One the partners we were training and flying alongside were the pilots of Pakistan. A Pakistani H-3 helicopter could be seen doing a hard over maneuver off the port side of the Connie. The H-3 helicopter is a helicopter the U.S. Navy no longer fly's because they fly the new H-60 helicopter.

The tempo slowed but it was enough to accommodate the training that was needed to maintain the pilot's quals, while making trek for a port of call in Singapore. The ship ties up with the fuel ship to take on fuel and supplies, while other stores are being brought on by helicopters pallet by pallets. Once in port downtown of Singapore could be seen from the flight deck and hanger bay of the Connie. The crew got dressed and waited in the berthing's because you couldn't hang out in the hanger bay unless your rank was called away over the 1MC. The security department always maintained orderly conduct of the crew coming and going off the ship. It made for a better time while you were in port.

Once in port we got to walk from shop to shop or take the subway downtown to go to the mall. The mall had several floors, and the main anchor of the mall was the bookstore and record shop. You had to go up and down several floors to get to see to whole store. I found a couple books on Scotland that I read during my off hours because sometimes the off hours can be long and boring. One thing of interest I got to see was the Merlion that looked out over the harbor, but it was obscured from view with a bridge the crossed in front of it. The bridge made the Merlion to be seen from out in the harbor. Once all personal was on board the ship.

The ship weighed anchor and got underway to continue on it trek toward home. Now that the ship was underway and the ship returned to its regular routine and the pilots readied for a day of flight ops. Before night check people could go to bed, a man overboard drill is called away over the 1MC. The man overboard drill is used to make sure all personal is back onboard after the ship has left the port. Once complete than the night check personal are allowed to go to sleep, so they can get ready for their

12 hour night shift. Flight ops got underway once the ship has secured from the man overboard drill. The plane captains got the plans ready for the flight ops and awaited the pilots to get into the planes that were on the flight schedule. Those would be the first ones to be launched when flight ops got underway. Laying there in our racks we could hear

and feel the flight ops get started and continue throughout the day.

It is a struggle to get something to work on when you are in corrosion, because at this point in the cruise all the shops are working on all the down planes in an effort to get them up. Because if the squadron can't get the plane up, the plane has to be craned off the ship once it reaches port. That is why a real effort is made to get the planes up and flyable status. Things got really busy once flight ops were secure for the night. Plane captains can be seen doing their post flight and daily checks on the planes. Once those checks were finished and things that need to be worked on by the shops get underway. The night time can get pretty busy for all the squadron's shops. Low and high power turns are done if needed to check the plane out or needed to get the plane up.

Keeping up the pilot's carrier quals are completed before the ship makes its next port visit. The on load of food stores, fuel and airplane fuel is brought on board by ship and helicopters and continues most of the day. The ships next port of call was Hong Kong but before we could get of the ship maintenance, and checks had to be completed before we could get off work. Port of calls were a much needed distraction from the day to day routine but it seemed like time slowed down. Time is the one thing we wanted to pass by when we have been away from home for so long, and couldn't wait to see our families again.

Once in Hong Kong the Connie anchored out in the harbor. Freighters from other countries can be seen anchored in the harbor. One the freighters I seen was flying a Norwegian flag. Security clears the hanger bay personal of the personal that are not suppose be in the hanger bay while they set-up up for the port visit. Even though we was in Hong Kong we ate at McDonalds and one thing different there is that they served beer there. I was able to find a computer their so I could check my e-mail, write email, and chat with my friends on my IM.

We were able to watch television and relax right there at the pier. You meet people there that you would have never met because of the crew's different working hours. I did get out in town to enjoy some local food and some shopping. The salt water smell was in the air as you walked around Hong Kong and you had to be careful where you walked and went around town. The alleys were narrow and the condos were close together. The crew knew once this port of call was behind the ship and then it was on our way home in a few weeks.

The ferry ride back to the ship at night, and the lights of the condos, apartments, and office building lighting up the shore line at night. The ferry could be felt bouncing up and down as it passed over each wave, and the salt water being blown on the boat. Feeling it hit you in the face and your body as we make are way back to the ship. Once back onboard ship we were preparing to pull out to sea. One way a night checker prepared to get back on the night shift was to stay up most or all night the last day in port. Once after the man over board drill you finally went to bed then. The Connie was now preparing to weigh anchor and get underway.

Once the Connie was underway the man over board was held, and the ship was back into the normal routine. A brief flight op schedule is started that way the pilots can maintain their quals. Once the flight schedule is complete the weapons are offloaded from the ship which runs around the clock. Weapons are being brought up from the magazines so that they may be sent up to the flight deck for off load to the supply ships. Stores from the supply ships are being on loaded along with JP-5 and fuel for the ship. Once the weapons are all offloaded from the ship on the way to Hawaii, and flight ops start up to get the pilots up to date with their quals. The Connie ties up with the supply ship to bring on fuel for the ship and JP-5 for the planes. Supply is also transferred from the ship along with being flown on board by helicopters. Now the crew prepared for the port visit in Hawaii after haven taken on the needed supplies.

The ship is pulled pier side and tied up to the pier. It is a much needed relaxation after such a long time away from states. It is nice being back in the states and quit the change from the foreign ports that we had visited. It had rain that morning when I had prepared to get off the ship and sun was behind a cloud and rays from the sun could be seen shining behind the cloud. I walk around the base and did some shopping for some music by Roxette. The ship with everyone on board prepared to depart Hawaii and head home.

The Connie was now headed home after it has departed Hawaii a few days ago. The planes being flown into the twin towers of the World Trade Center were a blow to the American way of life. These hits on our way of life were brought to us live by all of the news media outlets. They were played over and over again in the media. It also caused a mass panic in the population and a wonder what was going to happen next and where they were going to strike at the United States next. It was a horrific blow to our way of life, and several days later President Bush stood there at ground bringing the American and our allies in a rallying cry to fight against these people that could have carried out this attack on our way of life.

We were out to show these people that we would not bend to there well and shy away from it. It had been a long cruise and we were on our way home now. We were happy to be on are way home as we had been away from family, friends and our loved ones for six months. The ship and the crew prepared to pull into Hawaii for some much needed rest and to meet the love ones of the crew that had been flown over to Hawaii to meet them. One by one the family members were meet by their loved ones as they checked onboard, and after have checked in they were shown to where they would sleep.

This is also a time where the family members and dependents get live on the ship like their sons or daughters have for the last six months. They were hard metal beds and the mattresses we slept on were not very thick. Yes, are racks were very uncomfortable to sleep on. There was no way to seat up in bed because there was not much head room. We called them a coffin, and this is where we slept for the six month cruise. Then it was time to enjoy Hawaii and the time off that was well deserved. History was all around the ship and the crew. We were in a place that had been attacked by Japan, and that was a big blow to the west pacific naval fleet.

You could stand there and look over and see the *USS Arizona (BB-39)* Memorial. It was one the battle ships that was sunk in the attack on Pearl Harbor. In a fitting tribute, The *USS Missouri (BB-63)* was docked pier side just feet away from the *USS Arizona (BB-39)* Memorial. There was a lot to see on and off the base, and in the horizon you can see Aloha Stadium where the NFL Pro bowl is played and the University of Hawaii play football. It was great finally being back on American soil, and we felt a lot safer now. We have just enjoyed some much needed rest and relaxation and having gotten some shopping done before we had to pull back out to sea.

Now haven pulled back out to sea and now on our way back to ships home port in North Island. Now the crew gets a small taste of the life that we had to endure for the last six months. It is a life that we had chosen to lead. Very little maintenance was now getting done on the ship, but there was a lot of wondering around the ship by the families of the crew and the crew. Maintenance still wanted us to try and get some maintenance done, but it was not easy with people wondering around the hanger bay. There was a lot to see but it really didn't take long to see what there was to see. It was nice to enjoy the company of family and the change of pace that it offered a nice distraction after having been away from home.

One day was no different than any other day, but the only thing different was that we were on

our way home now. Things were about to change as we started a whole new day and as people woke up to the news of the morning. I was shocked like any other person that was watching the news that morning. I had just eaten breakfast in preparation for the day ahead. I stopped by the berthing and that is when I see the planes being flown into the World Trade Center. It was the only thing on peoples mind and what the people were talking about as you walked around the ship. The news was the only thing on around the ship trying to catch minute by minute what was going on with the attack on the United States.

The next thing we heard was that a plane had been flown into by a plane. Uncertainty and the unknown of what was going on and where and they were going to attack next. Flights now were being cancelled and flights being grounded now that airline travel was suspended till further notice by the President. Talk of the Government sending us back to the war zone had now started up, but we also had all of the crew's dependents and family now on board now. A lot of the crew did want to get in the fight against the enemy that did attack the United States. There was talk of all are post cruise leave being canceled to. On the news we heard that flight 93 had crashed into the ground in Pennsylvania. Flights may have been grounded but they still wanted to be prepared for whatever could or even might happen.

The scuttle butt and guessing of what was going on ran about the ship, and very few answers about what was going on came very slowly if at all. We did feel the ship speed up as if they were in a hurry to get back to home port in North Island. It was all people could talk about as they walked about the ship. The rumor was that they going to offload the family members and send the ship back out to patrol up and down the west coast. That is one the reasons that we heard for speeding to get into port.

The biggest question people had was," how could this have happened to the United States?" The people also wonder "why this had happened to the United States?" They being Al Qaeda had attacked are way of life once before as they wish to destroy the United States way of life. They have a hatred for our way of life and infidels that needs to be killed. The lack of communication is one thing from top to bottom and was one thing that feed into the rumors that were spread around the ship. Days went by before anything was ever said to us about what was going on and that we might be on call even if we were allowed to go on leave.

On our way back we picked-up an escort of gun boats that were carrying 50-caliber machine guns that were there to protect the ship. We watched the patrol boats keep other ships back away from the ship as we passed through the canal. It was along slow trek through the canal before we got to the dock. People could be seen, waving to us on the ship, lining the banks as we made our way through. Once back in port we offloaded the ship, but before that there was also the talk that we would be sent back to sea to patrol off of the west coast. We were allowed to fly back to our homeport in NAS Lemoore, CA.

Our family members were there to meet the planes as we all returned home. We were still on alert status even though we were allowed to go on leave. In the days after the attack on the United States, there was lots morning and questions the people sought answers for about why the country was attacked. Only once had the United States been attacked by a foreigner, that being Japan in World War 2

I had allowed my wife to use one of my MSN instant messengers, but she took the liberty of adding a friend to it. It was then I figured out what had happened, and why Snowy would not talk to me anymore. If she did do it, then she must have thought I would love my wife more for it. The exact opposite of what she must have thought took place for me. I had continued to explore, meet, and learn from lots of other people I had begun to talk with about things that were of interest to me. I have missed out on so much since I had been gone. There was much to catch up on now that I had gotten home from the cruise.

The United States Government finally found who was behind on the attack on our soil. Osama Bin Laden also had taken responsibility for the attack on the World Trade Center, The Pentagon and the plane crash in Pennsylvania. First responders shifted through the ruble of the World Trade Center, and the Pentagon for people that still might be alive and the bodies of the people that were killed. It was a long, tedious and painstaking process of digging and looking through that entire ruble of the buildings.

The digging in the ruble took day and night looking for people that were still alive that were trapped in the ruble of the twin towers. 1000's of people volunteered their time to the operation to found the people, and there were some people that were found alive in the buildings ruble. People even tried to recover their buddy's bodies of those that were killed in the twin towers. Lot of peoples that was killed their bodies were never recovered from the ruble of the buildings.

Days later President Bush paid a visit to the site devastation caused by the attack Al Qaeda on the World Trade Center. Then the President could see for himself the devastation that was caused by the attack of Al Qaeda. Standing there a top the rubble President Bush with mega phone in hand spoke to the crowd that had gathered at ground zero.

Saying that it would be a long and hard war, and that will not stop till we get the person's reasonable for this attack on the World Trade Center. They will soon hear from us, and with that war on terrier was declared. The United States and the countries NATO Allies mobilized to fight the war on terror and hunt down Osama Bin Laden and the people that were his allies and to punish them.

I had this long-term dream of owning my own business, but it had been hard to save and find the

money to fund my dream. I did try to get her to save, but she had to have it her way, and I gave into her as always. There was a lot of money that got spent by the both of us, wasted on needless things. That was my mistake to always to give in, but I did it to keep the peace in the house. It was after the first bankruptcy when her spending really got worse. I had asked her why the bills had got go and she told that me that "she could not keep up with the bills." The thing is, all she had to worry about was just the bills and the one child. Ulli and I had a friendship that had turned into an even better friendship, but she met another in the process. I had always enjoyed the long chats I had with Ulli. We used to talk a lot about things, but most of or our talks were about current political events that were taking place at the time.

Christmas was coming and I decided to incorporate what I had learned of the Norwegian Christmas traditions. That was along with buying one new Christmas ornament for each Christmas. I put up the Christmas tree ahead of time and was decorated with the help of my son. I baked seven different Christmas cookies, because that was one of my ancestor's traditions. I wanted this Christmas to remind me of our Norwegian Viking ancestors, and to share that tradition with my sons. I also shared some of the seven different cookies I had made with a couple of friends. Christmas Eve we would open one present, and the rest Christmas day. That is after I had put that out after the kids went to bed. The meals main courses is ham that dates back to the pagan Viking Customs. The ham, pig, was sacrificed to the Norse god Frøy. Christmas beer, in a horn, was dedicated to the Norse gods like Odin, Frøy, and Njord.

There are those people that you meet along the way that you grow to care about, but there is that special one you really want to get to know better. It had also come to that point and I need to save myself, and I wanted a divorce from my wife. I also knew my time in the U.S. Navy was coming to an end soon. I had to make that choice if I wanted to stay to the end or get out as soon as my time was up. It was in the meantime that I had gotten hurt by one person and another was about to enter my life very soon. She was a person who had become very special, and it was wonderful to spend the time we could together. It had reached that point, but we had to depart on my final cruise. But I was able to get a little time alone before I had to depart on a long cruise.

My Divorce

I moved a lot and not everything was moved with me. Every time I went home on leave I saw the stuff of mine that was left behind had been gone through by one of the wife's cousins. When I got home on leave I notice there was always something that I had turned up missing. I asked the wife about it and she never had an answer for why it was happening. There was no respect for my stuff that had been left at the wife's place and put into her aunt's storage. Amongst the stuff was things that I had kept since I was a kid, but is now gone. Since I was gone she chose what got packed-up and moved with us or was moved home to the new duty station. I was always on the move, so largely I didn't have a lot of time to deal with the stuff. This was just another thing that was there that ate at me like her getting in and reading my private e-mails. The respect for me as a person was their but as far as my stuff the respect wasn't there.

I did not trust my wife after that and had thought about getting a divorce, but I decided to try and work things out with her though. It was that day I turned to my wife and told her that there were two things that she cared about: herself and the money that I had made. I t was then that she told me how she loved and cared for me, but that fell on a deaf ear. I sometimes wish I had gone through with it much earlier as I look back on it. It was through the help of friends that helped us try to work things out, but even at that, I still did not trust her. It was during that time I went back to college as well. I was still working toward that degree.

It did reach that point where I finally decided to pursue a divorce. When I did, she had to be right there, but I am not sure why though. I think it was so that she could be in control of it all, and that everything would be on her terms. It was one of the many mistakes that I had made along the way. We had to go through counseling, and then when I went to see the lawyer she was right there, so after that, they could not help me out. She knew what she was doing the whole time when she did what she did. It was after that she got control over the paperwork and had filled out the information sheet that was used to produce the marital separation agreement. There was one day during our talks that she told me there is a time when you need to be selfish but that can be hard for me though because I have never been known as a selfish person.

The Move On

It turned out that I ended up getting hurt by Ulli as well. There were thoughts of suicide that entered my mind that night I had learned what had happened. I took several weeks because I thought Ulli was coming to see me, but I later found out she was with someone else. In the course of my hurting, I ended up meeting Kari, who lived in Michigan. She was to become a very special person to me, and we did get to spend some very special time together too. I made several flights from Los Angeles, California, to Michigan, where I got to spend some time with Kari. I did get to spend a wonderful and very meaningful weekend with her before I had to depart on my final cruise in the U.S. Navy. The weekend before I was to depart on my cruise I went to pick-up Kari from the airport. We spent the weekend together before I had to depart on my final cruise.

I was considered a geographical bachelor because I was still married yet. I was forced to move around a lot, and in that time I had many different roommates. I wanted to make my side look not so much like just the military. I had pictures in a frame and a couple of collector steins one I had gotten as a gift and the other I had bought. Well the one I had gotten as a gift which was a Budweiser stein gotten stolen. I would say the one roommate I had took it with him, because about the time he left is when it came up missing.

Second Cruise in VFA-151

I had to take care of a few things the morning I had to depart on a hop for San Diego, California, and the *USS Constellation (CV-64)*. It being my last trip in the navy, I decided to try to save as much money while I was on the cruise. I had also decided to set up a joint account with my girlfriend and had decided to have Kari transfer money out of my account and into the joint account. That way we would have the money for things to get us started in our new life together. Once the ship crossed the line and the ceremony was done, the ship weighed anchor in the harbor off Hong Kong.

Setting there in the harbor, you could the city light up and the lights reflecting off the water. The ship transited on to Singapore after we had stayed in Hong Kong for a few days. It was after a brief stay and on to the Gulf where the ship was to conduct operations. We had made a few ports of call in Bahrain, where security was tight, but I got to do some bowling, and I made a few phone calls to someone special. I also got to play around and send out a few e-mails to people. The e-mail was shut down for a while and the last port of call had been canceled.

The ship at least once a month got a briefing from the commander who over saw the Persian Gulf. The briefings were to advise us of what was happening with Iraq and what the ships role would be if the United States was to invade Iraq. The ship got extended in support of the war in Iraq, and the plans that were made had to be put on hold for another month. Night flight into the morning was started in support of Operation Iraqi Freedom. Laying there in my rack at night I could hear and feel the planes being shot off the catapults and the planes landing. It was also that seen reporters imbedded with the troops fighting their way to Bagdad, Iraq. Jeroldo Riviera got sent home because he got caught drawing the battle plan in the sand live on television.

The mail kept getting slower and slower but yet we had a lot of VIP'S that visited the ship. I

really wasn't big on the VIP's because I thought they were one of the reasons holding up the

mail besides the priority spare parts the ship had to have. I had also noticed how slow the other stuff she had sent me, when I looked at the post mark, had got to me. My girlfriend was going to mail me something out for Easter and the mail had gotten really slow by that time. I told her to keep it for me and I would get it from her when I had would come and see her after the cruise. E-mail was nice to have but there was still nothing like holding a letter in your hand from your loved one back home. I also really liked to get something in the mail as well. I guess that was a bit old fashion since we had e-mail at that time and it was a lot faster getting a letter from the person then as well.

It took three days to topple the Iraq government, but looting of the palaces and cities were being looted by the Iraqi citizens. Television showed one of our tanks pulling down a statue of Saddum Hussan. The military was not prepared for the chaos that the country descended into after the toppling of him and Iraq. Whether there was or weren't weapons of mass destruction we will never really know because of the entire looting, thief's and chaos that descended on the country after it fell. My girlfriend helped make my time pass by, and I was so happy to see the time pass by on a very routine cruise once released and able to make its transit out of the Gulf. The ship's crew and the air wing were able to enjoy some well-deserved time off in port at Fremantle, Australia. Now with the few well-deserved days off behind us, we continued on our way to Hawaii, where we were able to meet up with family and friends who were going to ride the ship the rest of the way to home.

While we were in port, I got to see something I knew I wouldn't get to see again any time. I visited the *USS Arizona (BB-39)* memorial before I got out of the military in a few months. The *USS Missouri (BB-63)* was moored just a short walk up the pier from the *USS Arizona (BB-39)* memorial. There are always those people you met along the way you become friends with and want to stay friends with, even when things are changing in your life. I was also able to spend some well-needed time with someone very special after I had returned home. We had gotten to spend even more time together in the days to come as my time in the U.S. Navy was drawing nearer to me retiring.

The movers came in packing up what I had left to be packed-up before my stuff was moved to Houghton Lake, MI. I had a lot packed-up, so it did not take long to move me. The day for my retirement was now here, and I got dressed in my best working uniform. I got to the conference room early that morning the day of the ceremony. Once there I was met by the Squadron Command Master Chief, and the other guest that were attending the ceremony. My Commanding Officer gave the key note speech for the ceremony followed by the presenting of the shadow box by the first class in charge of the first class mess. My skipper presented me with a squadron coin that he had in his pocket when he flew over Iraq and two spent 20mm cartridges that had been fired from one of the squadron planes. The first class was reading off the places I had been stationed, and most all the places I had been in the past were now decommissioned.

The first class turns to me and tells me gee your old I thought that was funny. I cut the cake and gave it out to all the people who attended the ceremony. The rest of my cake was taken to production control, so it could be shared with the rest of the men and women. Finally the time had come, and after the ceremony was behind me. I was able to beat foot out of town and on to a new life that I wanted to explore with someone very special. I had done a lot of planning ahead of time to make those final days run very smoothly, as my thoughts were now on the life that was laying ahead of me now. Every cruise I had made it seemed like I had missed out on a lot of things, and this one was even more special because it was the last cruise of my naval career. It also meant I got to spend even more time with Kari now that I was back home, and those were some special times for me. It gave me some time to get to know Kari even better.

Chapter 3

Life after the U.S. Navy

~ § ~

I was leaving the navy behind now that after my retirement ceremony was finished. I was in a hurry to get on the road since I had a long drive ahead of me. I had lots of time to think on my long cross-country drive to spend my first Christmas and a new life together with Kari in Michigan. My long days on the road were filled with thoughts of Kari, who I was about move in with. I raced down the highway toward my final destination after a snowstorm went through ahead of me and I kept track of the snowstorm that was coming in behind me.

I had kept in contact nightly with Kari as I progressed down the highway each day toward my final destination. I had finally arrived at my final destination, and saw Kari's oldest daughter out shoveling snow out of the driveway because it had snowed ahead of me. It was still a very special and wonderful day. I wanted to be there and to spend Christmas Eve with her. Kari waited for me to arrive, so that we may open the presents together. I had Kari some of her favorite music and some other special things. I got some new winter and a throw blanket that Kari had made.

Once I was settled in I had my stuff delivered to the house that was left packed in the garage. Which was a mistake because I didn't find out that a box got lost in the move. The box that was lot contained photo albums, school year books, some books, my sisters letters that I had kept and reread many times, and some material that I had gotten about a castle in Norway. It was too late for me to do anything about this box because I noticed it was missing too late to notify any one that it was missing.

The sad part though was my time there was filled with lots of mistakes all on my part. I was also ill prepared for life after the military and no plan other than to get a job. It had been a few months after I had arrived in Michigan before I was able to finally land that job with the Lear Corporation. I worked on the robot welders building the frames for automotive car seats. Things still were tense around the house, and in some ways that was my fault because I did fight with her. I was always on the job hunt since the job I had with Lear was never very secure. The layoffs from Lear always came at the worst of times, and I was ill prepared for the layoffs. I did also get another job but I only got paid on commission. There were some days that I wish I had kept that job because I would have learned more about something I wanted to learn more about that was the construction industry.

The snow can get deep and the streets can get very slick. There was one night I was coming home from town and I didn't have to go fast too slid on the slick roads. That night I tried to slow down, but I couldn't turn into the driveway because I was sliding on the road. There was a snow bank of snow that I had created from shoveling off the driveway and the sidewalks. They had been created on both sides of the driveway. Well I slid across the driveway and got my Pontiac Sunfire stuck on the snow bank. I tried to dig it out but I wasn't getting anywhere. A person that had been driving by who had been plowing out driveways drove by the house, and had seen the predicament I was in. In the mean, Kari had come out to see what had happened and to see who I was talking to. He asked if he could help me but I had no choice but to agree. We also agreed to let him plow out the driveway.

Things had end between and Kari and I had to move home. It was my fault that it ended the way it did. I hugged Kari and Emily good bye and then I got in my car. The drive home was sort of boring, so I took my time to get home. My first stop on my trip home was Illinois. Morning had come and now I was back on the road headed for home. On the way I had found a shop, and I decided to stop since I wasn't in a big hurry to get home. Driving into Nebraska I decided to stop at the same place

I had stopped at coming to Michigan, but I didn't find it. I had to stop somewhere else in Nebraska. My next stop was Rock Springs, WY, and then it was on to home. It did give me a lot of time to think about what had happened back in Michigan and to put everything that had happened in perspective.

Chapter 4

Returning to New Plymouth, ID

~ § ~

I had been living with Kari for about a year and half and now I was back at home living with my mom. Looking back at my life with Kari, one day stands out in my mind most of all. We got to spend the day together at the Renaissance fair. It was a place built like a medieval village, with lots of people in costumes from that period of time. One of the highlights of the fair was the real jousting tournament that was held between different competitors from different parts of the world. Even though things ended after she kicked me out, but that was because I couldn't stop arguing with her. I actually get along with her better than my ex-wife now. There was a person that told that was because I didn't have a lot of bad feeling with the ex-girlfriend like I did with the ex-wife. Even though things didn't work out there, we are still friends, which is nice with me.

There were several others afterward, but all ended in a disaster as well. What made things hurt even worse was these were some people I had been talking to for years before I had met them in person. I have tried to learn from all these mistakes, but I still end up making the same mistake again in the end. I had been digging myself into a hole financially during this time as well because I wanted to live the life I had wanted. The gas prices had been going up at the same time, which was making it tough to make a living as well. The reason I kept falling short was because I had child support services in my pocket each month. I still have that long-term obligation to deal with for a while.

I had been bouncing around between jobs as I look for a full-time job and none of the jobs were for me. The jobs were not me and not what I was looking for. One thing I did after work, I spent a lot of my free time online just chatting before I decided to join this one adult online dating site. I met a lot of wonderful people from different parts of the United States and even different parts of the world. I met Teri, Cami, Sharla and Mari in real life after talking to them for a little while. The biggest drawback is that I live too far from a lot of the people these I had talked to online. One of the persons I had met from online, and she proceeded tell me that I was too skinny.

It had been almost two years since I had talked to Shannon, and in those two years many things had changed for her. I had enjoyed talking to her, and wanted to get to know her better. I got my chance to reconnect with Shannon once more after things didn't work out for her and the guy she had married. I could not wait to get to know her better, and I did finally get that chance to meet her in person. I had my reservations though because I was coming on the heels of this other meeting I had with Sharla, which was a bust for me.

I had talked to Shannon for a few months prior, but it had been a few years since I had talked to her last. I did finally get to meet Shannon, and even though I had a lot of apprehension prior to my meeting with her. I made known my apprehension about meeting her, but she really wanted to meet me. Shannon talked me into to meeting with her that weekend, because I was ready to back away from meeting her. We were to meet, talk and get to know each other and nothing more than that. I really wanted to meet her as well, and I completed the plans to meet her. I am glad that I got to meet her finally, but a lot of emotions came into play. Those emotions that I felt has led to all the regrets I feel in how the weekend ended. I just wish it would have turned out differently than it did, but she will always be a special person to me. How it ended will always be the biggest regret I will always have, and I have learned from it. I have moved on and have used the lessons I had learned from it. I am a lot more skeptical about the things that people tell me. It has also caused me to think about meeting people since then, and in a lot of ways it has made me more reluctant to step outside myself and meet people.

There was this other one that told me I lived too far away from her. I had started chatting with Alisa who wanted me to check out her profile on this other adult dating site, but I had to join it first. It ended though as she has met another person that she had known before. During the time I had spent on this other site, I got to know some other people. In the course of my time there I had gotten to know this one other person along with several other people. There was one who I enjoyed talking to and spending time with Kat, Jamie, Kitty, Missy, Whitney and all others that I met there.

Spending time with them always seemed to make the end of the day feel just a little bit better, but there was this one special person who I had met along the way who could brighten my day with her smile. Along the way, I had met a few people who had found that special place in my heart. There was that special one that meant even more to me in a lot of ways, but there was that one mistake that I made in search of an answer I was looking for. I had made a few other mistakes along the way, and one of these mistakes was a big one that hurt the person's feelings badly. It hurts me when I lose a friend and when they won't talk to me anymore.

Sometime later I made another mistake that got me put in jail and that cost me a lot as well. That was one mistake that I have regretted and has cost me a lot in many ways. I have regretted it a lot ever since it had happened to me. It still feels like I hurt those ones that are close to me in some way even though I don't mean to and that hurts me too. I have been working hard to turn my life around in a more positive and constructive way, but I still have this self-destructive way of putting myself down. I need to move past that and be more positive on myself, so otherwise I need to change my whole mindset.

The both of us used no common sense whatsoever in the amount that I was to pay her. It was that lack of thought that I am still living with today, and for a while as they are still young yet. I really didn't give it much thought in how much it was going to cost me, because I wanted to get rid of her. Not caring how much it was going to cost me was my biggest mistake, now that I look back at it. The other bad part is with Oregon, they changed the law to, and now I will be paying child support till the youngest one is twenty-one. The amount was fine while I was in the navy, but it was after I retired from the navy that I ran into problems with paying the amount that I was ordered to pay her. I could not do anything since I did not have the judgment before I had retired for the service. One thing I have learned since then is that it was a mistake for her to have gotten control over all the paperwork. She did hold on to it to until I had finally retired, and I hated her for that. She did that so she could get the benefits, so here she is again, thinking about herself.

It has been a rough and rocky road since I had divorced my ex-wife. I did finally get what I am paying her lowered, but the damage was done already. I am still living with what had happened because I had fallen behind in the payments, and now they are lifting money out of everything I get. That has made things tough for me to put money toward making my dream a reality. I have wanted many times to just throw up my hands and calling it quits. Saying she had won yet again, but I can't let her do that though. I had let my wife win one too many times before in our married life, and I am fighting hard to not let her win yet again. I have been working hard to make my dreams a reality but her and our fine government have been making that so very tough. The government is making it tough because every time I file my income taxes they take time and give it to the ex-wife. I will find a way to overcome it, and make my dream of a better life a reality.

The one long-time dream that I had was to start my own business. It was one day while I was watching *Oprah*, and I was sitting there listening to them as they talked about power of the mind. They talked about how forces of attraction are related to how you could get out of debt. They had talked about writing an essay about how your life looked like if I was out of debt. One day I sat down taking a look at it. I had been reading one of Donald Trump's books where he talks about if you are going to dream then you should dream big. I started thinking about this dream I had of starting my own business and I wanted to start it for all the right reasons after all I had been in my private life. I had proceeded to write it out that night, so as I was seating there one day when I wrote this:

How I imagined my life.

The life I imagine if I was debt free and what would my life be like afterward. I would be able to invest in IRA, that would have stocks and a mutual fund in it. My cash position builds, so that would give me a greater cash presence. Once I have that I would then be able to invest in the good real estate deals as they do come along.

That way I could build condo, hotels, office buildings, and houses along a golf course, along with vacation houses in nice places around the country for fractional vacation homes. Casino resort hotels so that would further expand my wealth. As my wealth grows, so will the money I give to charity. It would also give me the resources to go to Norway, where I could view the castles built by the Vikings. I would enjoy the night life that the country had to offer, and being able to take a train or a ferry ride around the country.

A changing of the corner.

I had written this while I was taking courses from Trump University and reading books that were written by Donald Trump and Robert Kiyosaki. Since I had written that I have been saving and investing 10 percent of income, plus I had been adding more when I could. I have also created a budget that would create a surplus to my budget. I have started a business entity, which I will be adding my brokerage to it. I will soon be blending several different business entities together to protect my assets. I have approached stock investing with cost value as a way to invest in stocks and bonds. I am also working with small business development on putting together a business plan for my business. Soon, I will be going to college, where I will be taking business courses.

I have also come to realize that I need to get over my fear of failure, and that it was holding me back from fulfilling my dream of owning my own business. I need to change my attitude and everything about myself doubt and self-confidence that I have about myself. It is the one thing that is the hardest to change because I have lived with those self-doubts about myself for a very long time. The other thing is that I need to do and that was that I needed to slow down and not push quit so hard at things. I think that is a lot of where the cause a lot of my problems. I do remember what my uncle had said long ago about not wanting it all at once but to take my time. I have broken down my dream into small parts. These small parts would feed the larger part of the picture. I need these small parts to produce an income for the overall business I am building. It is the only way I can do it since I am at a handicap due to what I let happen. I am not letting that keep me from living out my dream, and living that dream would be the one thing that would be the greatest change in my life.

Even after I have changed the corner on my life I still sometimes dream of the past and some of it is good and happy but the other part of it is sad cause it is of the mistakes I had made in my life. I think about the people I had enjoyed talking to along the way. The bad things and the things that have gone wrong in my life seem to dominate my thoughts and even my dreams. I sometimes wish I was that carefree kid again because I miss those days.

I grew up going to church every Sunday morning and even attended services in the evening. I had been pretty active in the church back then. I was and usher and had been appointed as a jounior deacon for the church. There were a lot of things I had lost growing up and sometimes you are forced to grow up to fast. I had lost that young naïve person that grew up on the farm in Idaho pretty fast, and into one that was more street wise. I am one who doesn't accept a lot of things at face value and I tend to look more at what their actions is telling me.

I was laying on my bed one night thinking and watching Highlander: The end game when I got to thinking about what they were saying. It had gotten me to think about a few things that have happened in my past. Hurting them was something that happened and I have regretted it ever since it had happened. I do wish I could set it right with them, but we no longer talk to each other. Maybe one day I will be able to make it right with them both, but maybe when the time it is right it might happen. Until that time I will continue to work on me and bettering myself. In a lot of ways, the movie resembles my life over the past few years. I remembered Shannon liked the highlander series, and in the movie it stared one of the main characters from the television series.

I had to take charge of my own and I looked at it as if there was no one there to help me through what was going on in my life financially. I kept telling myself that I didn't want to file bankruptcy and somehow I could get them all paid off over time. I was fooling myself, and that I was too far in debt. I had to face that fact of how much debt I had, and file bankruptcy. It is not the end of the world, but it can be if you don't change things afterward. There are a lot of people who have had to file again and again cause of poor money management.

The changing started even before the bankruptcy was behind me. I had started to keep track of what I was spending for a month. That meant even keeping track of what I had spent for the month. It was with that information that I had collected over the month. I took that information and worked out a workable budget that created savings into the budget. I had also wanted to put those dollars that I was saving to work for me, but I also wanted to protect those assets as well. That is when I started to find and talk to different discount brokerage firms, and then I came across one that dealt with the military personal. It is also run by ex-military personal, and me being ex-military as well. It made it all that much nicer to deal with a place that caters to ex-military and their family. That is why I have most all accounts with them. They had all I wanted in a discount brokerage firm. Once I had the account set-up with them. I also wanted to protect those assets.

I read a book written by J.J. Childers, J.D. who is a lawyer that specializes in asset protection. I had heard about to many people who had lost their wealth to being sued by a predator, and I didn't want to be one of those people. That is when I set-up a limited liability company, and transferred ownership of the investment account to Strom Capital Investments LLC. I wanted to write a book about my life and tell people about my struggles, and how I never gave up on my dreams. I also wanted to tell people what I had learned financially. I wrote a book about finances that way I could pass on what I had learned about finances. I did make a Limited Liability Company owner of the copyrights to the books that I wrote. Mjollnir Capital LLC owns all the Copyrights to the books that I write, and they are sold through the Olsen Organization. The first book I titled, "Always Aware: The journey of my life", was a book about my life.

An LLC may not be a company in its formation but that doesn't mean it can't be treat as a company. Following a lot of the formalities of a company can help you from having the veil of the LLC pierced. Not following the formalities can be the easiest way to have the veil of the LLC pierced. Once it is pierced it could cost you your liability protection and lots of money. Protection of your assets is the one thing you want from the predators that want to take it away from you.

New Plymouth still hadn't changed much since I had been away. It was a town that was built around farming. The young people who and have lived here wanted more than just farming. Lots of them moved away in search of other opportunities that they couldn't be found in New Plymouth. I looked at the town thinking about how the town could be lots more that it is. The mayors of the town either wanted to keep the town as it is or the mayors were in the office for themselves and didn't do much to better the town as a whole.

There was one mayor who did supply a few jobs for the town, and had built a brand new three-story building. He had also bought up a majority of the building downtown. He is one the few mayors that helped the town and helped himself.

Spinning out of control

I had decided to go back to college full time and pursue getting my degree that I had been working on what seemed to be a life time. My resources had grown over the last year or so, and I felt it was time to find someone to help me out. I did have a lot of homework to do, and I didn't have the kind of time I needed to do the books. I also knew a friend who needed some help financially, so I decided to hire her as my bookkeeper. I wanted to do things the right way and above the board. I also had an interest in making things and then trying to sell them over the internet.

I got my state sales tax ID number, and also had gotten my unemployment ID number set-up with the state. I still lacked Workers Compensation coverage, and that would prove to be the toughest thing of all. My biggest mistake was to hire the person before I had everything in place, and because she worked out of her home for me. Workers Comp. here in the State of Idaho considered her high risk, and couldn't be covered by the state fund. I found that out from a representative from The Insurance Group and State Farm. Tammi from The Insurance Group helped me in filling out the needed paperwork.

I found out some background on why and how Workers Compensation in the United States came about. England in 1897 repealed the employer's liability act of 1880, and replaced it with the Workmen's Compensation Act. Meanwhile, the storm that swept through Europe during this period of industrialization reached the shores of the United States it was fueled by the aftermath of the Civil War from 1861 to 1865. Work place injuries became more common in the aftermath of the industrial revolution. A huge number of people took manufacturing jobs. While working in the factories, these employee's would often be injured from the heavy machinery or other hazardous work conditions.

The United States used the European model for when they were to finally enact Worker's Compensation Law of 1911. Wisconsin was the first state to adopt the law, and by 1948, every state had some form of Workmen's Comp. I essence, this social program is a pact between employers and employees. Employers are mandated to cover medical care and provide wage replacement for injured workers, in exchange for this protection, the workers compensation becomes the exclusive remedy for workers. Although the courts have upheld this doctrine for nearly a century, in some instances, such as willful intent or bad faith, court challenges have succeeded in piecing the exclusivity to the workers.

In the meantime, I had decided that I wanted to work on making Viking and Norman shields that I wanted to sell online. I needed help in getting the online store set-up, and I had found a website to host it. I needed a web developer to help me build the web site. I was trying to do this, so that I would have money coming in to pay for my business expenses for Bohus Properties. I had chosen the name because it was a Norwegian fortress that had never been defeated in combat even though it was later seeded to the Kingdom of Sweden as per the Treaty of Roskilde also cause of their union with Denmark.

I found all of the parts and plans that I needed to make the shields with, but I still hadn't found a web designer to build my web site. I went to the small business development center and got some names of web designers. In the meantime, with all of my searching for a person to build my web site and the set-up for the sells, and shipping of the products that I was interested in selling. I was trying too hard to speed it along but the slower it all seemed to go.

Remember I told you I had trouble in getting my Workers Comp. set-up well I hadn't as of yet. It was at that time I got a call from a person who worked for the State of Idaho Worker's Comp. division. He had some questions for me on weather I had gotten workers comp as of yet, and if I had any employee's working for me at the time. I told him yes I had one, and all the information relevant to her. While that was going on I had set-up with my mom's help at Ladco leasing who did the credit card processing. They were sub-contracted by Key Bank online merchant services. I still didn't have the web site in place yet when I had gotten this set-up, and now I was paying them plus the bank for its payroll services, merchant services and bank service charge fees.

I still had no money coming in, but I had lots of money going out now. The web site was taking forever and it never did get built. I had then gotten a letters from the workers comp. board telling that I was going to be fined $25.00 a day for each day I didn't have workers comp. insurance. I finally got my workers comp. in place. I was already hurting for money, and the problems just begun to mount. I had to make a deal with the State of Idaho to pay off Workers Comp. fines monthly. I also had to take a judgment against me and the business for those fines. There was still no online business yet, and I had all these expenses mounting I had to make a choice and I had to make that choice fast.

Pulling back from the edge

I did expect to lose some money when I had started all of it, but it was getting to where I was losing more money than I had expected and fast. I had gone through about all I have saved up to that point. I had a very big choice to make and the decision was to cut loses at that point and move on from there. I was being very pragmatic in my choice to dissolve Bohus Properties Company and Stone Meadow Lawn Care. Neither one of them was making any money, but they had cost me lots of money in expenses and fines. I took what little I had left and invested it in Strom Capital Investments LLC. The bleeding of my capital had at least stopped for a while.

I wanted more, but I had gone to fast in what I wanted to do. I was doing this with what little financial means I had available to myself. I didn't fully research and plan out what I wanted to do, and how much it would cost me financially. I also didn't take in account the time and the problems that I was going to run into along the way. I had reached the point where I couldn't absorb the loses and I had to get back to the point that was working for me. Expanding was a good idea if everything fell into place in a timely manner. I got back to my core business I was building, and that was saving and investing my money. I was doing pretty well since the stocks and bonds were on the rebound after the crash in the stock market.

There was one thing yet to come, and that was Ladco Leasing. One the biggest things I had done wrong with them and that were I should have read the contract more carefully then I had. It was all in a haste to get the online business up and running. The online business never did get off the ground, and now I was stuck with a service I couldn't use now. I had also leveraged my mom's good credit in doing this. Being in a haste and not being more careful about things and on a limited budget can lead to bad things happening as I was about to find out. One huge thing I was about to find out about Ladco leasing and the contract that we had signed with them after I had already fallen behind in my payments with them.

I found out from one the representative that the contract with them was non-cancelable contract that we had signed with them. I was trying to catch up my bill, but it was too late because the next thing I knew they had turned it over for collections. The collection company said I owed Ladco $1,600.00 and that I hadn't made any payments to them for 3 or 4 months. I had to make a deal with them to pay it off monthly. What got me mad about the whole deal was I had paid them some but that didn't matter to them and cause I had put mom's credit on the line as well. They had me over the barrel their! Once they were paid off I was done with them. I could get back to saving and investing now that I didn't have Ladco Leasing to pay for.

Now with that behind me I could get back to work on my college homework. I could also get back to rebuilding my personal brand the one I had let come known as a quitter and a person that couldn't be counted on. That isn't what the Navy had taught me, and it wasn't something that my

parents had taught me. They taught me how to show-up on time, be dependable and reliable. I

need to work hard at rebuilding and transforming my personal brand into something that is positive and truly reflects the person that I truly am. It all begins with the core values I was taught by my parents and that was reinforced by the Navy. I have started that change with my college classes and my studies.

A disaster can be good or bad, but it is how you handle the disaster in the end. How you handle the disaster can make or break your success. I still kept my focus on what I wanted and pushed ahead toward the goals I had set for myself. I have always been one of focus and determination especially when it comes to known what I want out of life. The true test and measure of the person and what they are made of is how they can handle the setbacks that come their way. The lessen's I learned from my earlier failures of Bohus Properties and Stone Meadow Lawn Care, and their failure gave rise to the Olsen Organization LLC.

The OLSEN™ brand

I gave a lot thought about choosing to name my business after myself. At first I wasn't going to do and I wanted to be different from what had already been done, but I came back and did name the business after myself. A successful brand is made up of two parts. The first being your own personal brand, and the second being what your business brand stands for. The public's view of your personal brand can make or break your business brand.

I do think about my dad, Albert, and I do wish he was still here with me. I wish he was here to help me build the business. His guidance would be such a great help and a much needed ear to confide in. Even though he said I wouldn't amount to much. He was a man I looked up to very much and wanted to be like in so many ways. I do think my dad, Albert, would be proud of me what I have built and done so far in my life and business. I took what I learned in my new book "Olsen: My financial journey", and put to work in building the Olsen Organization LLC. Investing in other businesses is part of the business, but the main focus is real estate and the development of the real estate. That is what led me to deciding to buy into the El Paso, Texas area. It took me a while to decide on the right piece of ground to buy. I was also thinking big

when I decided on the piece of ground I was buying.

The collapse of the real estate and financial markets of 2008 have made it tough to get into real estate development. Working with partners is going to be more important to accomplishing the goals I have set out for the business. There has been a steady reshaping of the business over this last year and I will keep reshaping it as I go along in the building of the Olsen™ brand. The Olsen brand is a family brand, and a family business that will take in account the different family personalities. I want to make it a business that my dad would have been proud of. It is an ongoing building process, like learning there is always something new to learn, to build something special.

Many the things I learned and wrote down in the second book I published just this year. Putting many of those things to work for me in the things I have chosen to invest in. They were good solid companies that have been in business many years and have a good and solid performance record behind them. My company owning the investment account in a way to protect it against predators and great tax advantages as well. Making money and protect what you want to build it against the predators who want to take your assets you have built up away from you. If I lose money in the company I can write it off against my taxes.

You want to make money and not give it away to one the biggest predators, that being the U.S. Government. Why let them take your money and spend it when you can keep as much of it as you legally can. You know how to use your money and invest your money to make more money.

I have read and I have followed a lot of what Warren Buffet said about investing my money. I even followed him into the stock market when everyone one was selling and getting out of the stock Market. The Olsen Organization will be made up of multiple entities blended together to form the asset protection. Olsen Book of Olsen Organization will hold the licensing and sales rights to books, while Mjollnir Capital owns the Copyrights of the intellectual and Trade Marks. Strom Holding will hold the undeveloped land, houses and commercial buildings awaiting remodel. Olsen merchandise made up of Olsen Candles selling candles and Bohus Viking's branded Viking and Norman Shields. Olsen Office Branded book cases and desks made of poplar.

Warren Buffet's 10 rules to get rich

Rule one is reinvesting your profits, which for me is to have my dividends reinvested in the stocks and bonds.

Rule two be willing to be different, and I was willing to buy when everyone was selling in good quality stocks.

Rule three never suck your thumb and in other wards make up your mind and act in a timely manner.

Rule four spell out the deal before you start, because you have greater leverage before you start the deal.

Rule five watch the small expenses because those small expenses can add up fast, and then you won't realize where all your money went to.

Rule six limit what you borrow because those interest costs on what you borrow won't make you rich.

Rule seven be persistent with a plan be unique and different than your competitors.

Rule eight know when to quit, and walk away from the deal because you could lose more money than you would have to.

Rule nine assess your risk because that risk could outweigh the benefits you would gain.

Rule ten know what success really means and success means different things to different people.

I looked for good quality stocks that I knew and had good value to them. The portfolio I had constructed with USAA was one of good quality and value to them.

My portfolio
Novo-Nordisk A S NVO
Statoil ASA STO
Deere & CO DE
Wells Fargo & CO WFC
Nucor Corp NUE
Nordic American Tankers NAT

Suburban Propane Partners LP SPH
Energy Transfer Partners LP ETP

USAA short term bond fund USSBX

My latest acquisition to my portfolio was USAA precious metal fund.

Creating a budget to make you rich and invest your assets to make more money. Leveraging your money is another good way to accumulate even more assets. It is a form of good credit that puts money into your pocket instead of taking money away from you. Image in business and in life are very important to how successful your business will be. That includes what you post to your facebook page because you never know who is looking at any of those social media sites.

I actually found out the hard way and after I had did what I did and tried to correct my mistake. It was too late really because by the time I took action to correct the damage had already been started to my image. I actually lost a very good friend over it but she has since forgiven me for it and now we are talking again. You may think what you are doing, and posting to those social media sites is harmless. You may think it is not harmless, but you never know who might view your social media page. You never know how people might take what you say on one of the social media sites.

JOHN AND SONS LARS AND JAMES

2003 WEST PAC CRUISE US NAVY

GRADUATION 1980

YOUNG JOHN

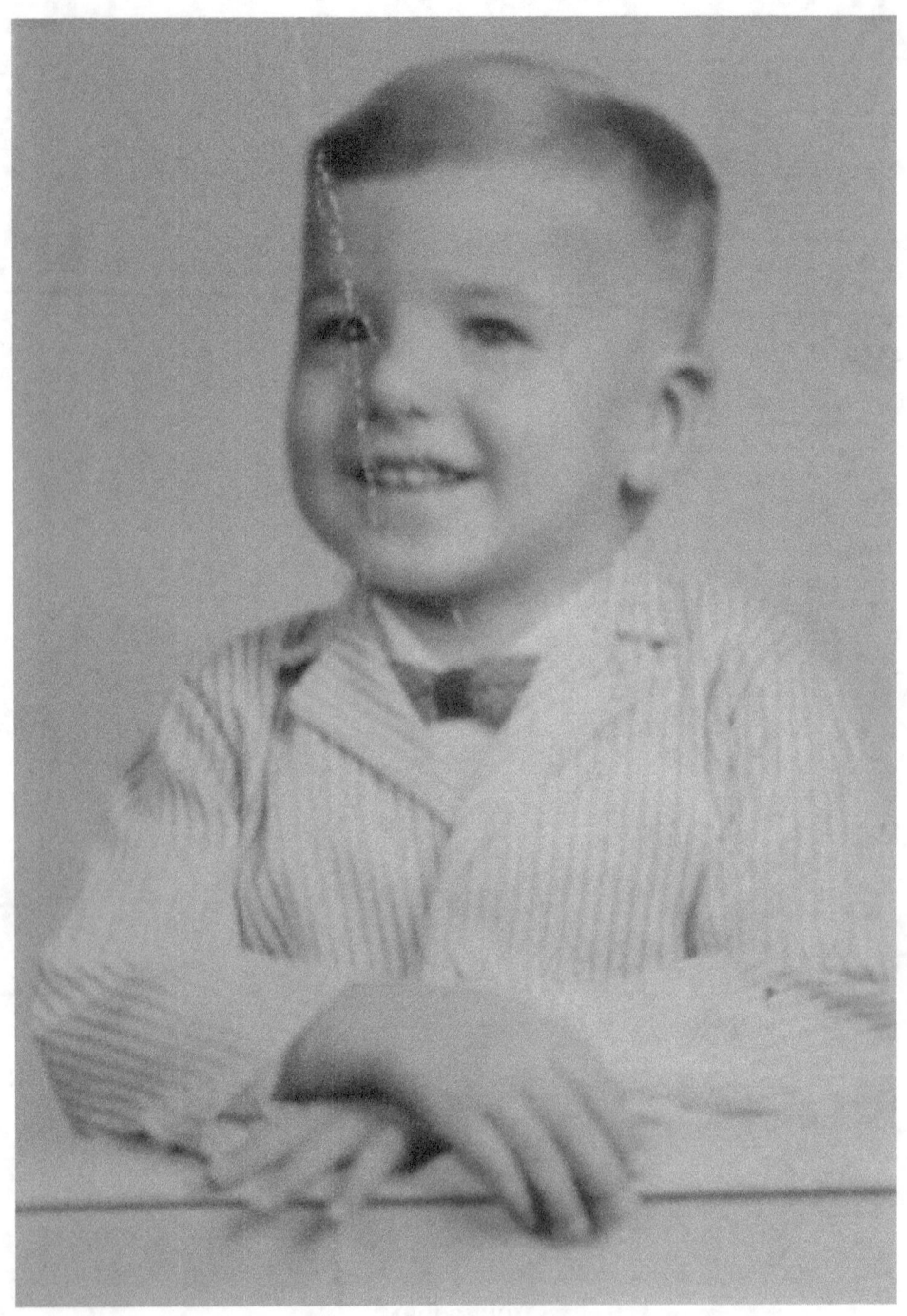

JOHN

JOHN SLEEPING IN CORNER AT MOM'S FRIEND'S HOUSE

JOHN IN YARD AT GRANDMA'S HOUSE

JOHN AND MOM

MY DAD ALBERT

My mom Viola

Chapter 5

Olsen Hidden Ranch, El Paso, TX

~ § ~

I read in local newspaper that there was foreclosed property for sale in El Paso, TX. I did some research on the internet on property that was for sale. I thought long and hard about the property that was for sale in El Paso, TX. I had to believe the company I was dealing with was real and that I wasn't getting taken by them. I saw the property as a good investment, but I kept on looking for that one right piece of property.

Once I had finally found that right piece of property. I downloaded and printed out the land property agreement to purchase a piece of ground in the El Paso, TX area. I didn't have any negotiations with the owner of the property. I had a few ideas for the property while looking at several magazines that contained blue prints of different houses. I did decide on a house that I would love to build on the land.

Choosing a building site means everything to your overall comfort in the house. There should be no surprises when you do move into the house unlike a home that was built in Rexburg, ID. It was a five bedroom house that was priced at $180,000.00 and Mr. Sessions and his wife thought it was a steal at that price. The snakes released a foul smelly musk into the water. Mr. Sessions killed 42 snakes in one day. They found out to their surprise the house was infested with thousands of Garter Snakes.

It was noted in the documents that the Sessions but they thought of it as a way for the previous owners to get out of the contract and in the end the walked away from the house themselves. The bank found out that the house had been built on a snake bed, but they tried to resell the house. The bank did finally pull it off the market once Animal Plant had aired a story about the house on their network. Some of those surprises can also cost you big money like it did in Meridian.

Those costs came to millions of dollars. The owner still has oversight of the project and even keeps your hand in the project even if you had appointed a project manager. You as the owner of the project mean you are still in control of the project that is one thing you never give up. That is like a supervisor in a business who delegates a task to be done by a co-worker. The supervisor still ultimate responsibility of the task even though he has delegated it out to a co-worker.

I am going to college at ITT-tech. Institute. I put to use the skills that I have been learning in my classes to use in designing the house that I would have loved to build on the property that I was buying. I did it as part of a class project. The class was designed to teach me about architecture and what goes into designing the house. The building codes I had to follow when designing the house. The building codes are there to protect the persons living in the house and the building inspector has to sign off on the building permit saying that you followed those building codes and that the building is safe.

The class instructor, Miss Earl, gave out the design parameters of the house we needed to design as our class project. This was designed as a real life scenario that we would meet as a client and designer. Listening to the client and incorporating the client's wishes is an important part of the design process. The parameters of the project were what I used in designing my house for my Architecture 1 class that I needed to take for my Computer Drafting & Design degree.

The project was a 1500 to 2000 sq. ft. one story house. A married couple with one child and expandable if needed in the future. A Family room and kitchen big enough to accommodate parties and social get together. The house I decided on was a three bedroom, two and a half bathroom and was almost 2000 sq. ft. one story house. A large two car garage that measured 20 ft. x 25 ft. The project also allowed me to be both the client and the designer, which allowed me to design a house that I would love to build for myself.

Money problems didn't allow me to keep the land I had to turn it back to Sunset Ranch, but I will try again one day. I still have the plans for the house I would like to build.

Civil drafting is one of my classes in Computer Drafting and Design that I am taking to get my Associate of Science. The house I designed for the land in El Paso. I took it and added to the site plan that I designed. I can see how the house would have looked on the land that I was purchasing in El Paso, TX.

The house and site can be designed, so it meets the LEED qualifications. It would be a great location for green energy because it has no energy source being the property is out in the country.

Chapter 6

Olsen Ash Meadow, New Plymouth, ID

~ § ~

It is the house that my parents, Albert and Viola Olsen Jr., had finally bought after a life time of renting the house they had raised their family in. Mom really enjoyed the house but dad got sick shortly after they moved to town. Dad really didn't get to enjoy the house they had finally bought because he passed away a few short months after he had gotten sick. Mom has now passed away and now the bank has foreclosed on the house. I decided to look for a house to buy, and talked to a couple different real estate agents. This was one the houses the real estate agent had shown me, but I didn't buy it cause I later went into the military.

If I was able to purchase the house it would be for sentimental reasons. I feel that my parents' house should be kept in the family, but I haven't been able to accomplish it as of yet. I haven't given-up on that yet, and am still working toward acquiring the house. It is just going to be a while before it happens.

Remodeling and expanding the house by 5 to 10 feet on all four sides would give me to do a lot more with the house. The complete lawn needs to be tore up, and redone to get rid of morning glory, and other weeds. I had started to redesign and do the lawn, but there is still a lot of work needs to be done on the lawn. It would make for a better house as well. There is a real upgrading of the house needed as well.

One the first things I would do is get rid of the ceiling heat throughout the house. Then the next thing I would do is put in air conditioning throughout the rooms. It would be a greenhouse that would qualify as a LEED house. Replacing the windows throughout the house would be the next thing that we be accomplished. Each of the rooms in the house would be made bigger. All of the flooring would be tore up and replaced. A bathroom in the master bedroom would be added and the other bathroom redesigned and remodeled.

Lighting of the rooms will be needed, and there is no lighting in the family room. A kitchen made bigger, so you can do a lot more in. Parties and family gatherings are something that I like to do. It would be made easier with a bigger kitchen and dining room. Family gatherings are one of the things my parents loved, and it also gave my parents a way to stay in touch with the other family members. There are other things that I would like to do to this house. It is the big and little things that could make this a special place to own.

Using what I have learned in my computer drafting and design classes to redesign the house. I have laid out some of my thoughts for the house on paper, but I have yet to lay it out as a blueprint showing how the house would look once redesigned. Working with family could make it work out, and it will work. Working with family and friends also could help in the purchase of

the family house. I have also thought about renting out the house after its purchase. Family also could help me in redesigning the house as well. It may be something that the family could be proud of. There is information I will also need to obtain from the title company. This information will help me in drawing up the plans for the house.

Once planned out it would have to be taken before the city gov't and building permits would have to be obtained. It will all be done once the house has been acquired, and that is one thing I have not given up getting done.

Chapter 7

A week in my life

I am an early morning riser, and my day begins by reading the USA today, the Norway Post, Irish times, Ice News, and the Jersey Evening Post. Then taking a mile walk after I turned on the today show and making a pot of coffee. A relaxing walk prepares me for the work ahead of me that day. Having got ready I head to work at 8:45, and having arrived at work. I check on how the stock market is doing that day. Once ready I went about my days work.

Monday 14 May 2012
0900 Left for ITT-Tech Institute to work on class work for my college at 6 pm. It is a class that will help me prepare for life after college.
1200 Made a phone call a job in Payette who was looking for a part time CAD-Tech. Went back to work on my homework for my Portfolio class.
1pm Called USAA to talk to a financial advisor about my portfolio I hold with them. Talking over another financial matter with them that could help me grow my money and pay off my debts that I owe.

Tuesday 15 May 2012
0900 Worked on homework for CAD class. Am designing a Rec./ Educational center. That I have thought about building sometime in New Plymouth. It will look great with a mixed building that I had designed in my Architecture class. I have the piece of ground that I would love to build the buildings on. I am thinking how New Plymouth can be more that it is right now.

1200 I drove to New Plymouth and helped Martina with her homework. I continued to work on my homework, and showed her what I had been working on in my CAD class.

Wednesday 16 May 2012
0900 called different dealerships that had cars for sale. I did set-up to look at a car. I worked on homework for my CAD class.
1200 look at more dealerships for a car and made a phone call to my niece Martina for a ride. I also filled her in on what was going on with my car.

Thursday 17 May 2012
0900 Left with my niece Martina to go look at the car I had decided on, but I was informed that the car I was to look at had an engine problem. I looked at a different car, but didn't get that car.
It took me most all day and tried different ways to get the car but in the end it still didn't work out in my favor.

Friday 18 May 2012
0900 I left for school so I could work on homework that I needed to get done for the class I had that night. I also needed to get the homework for the class I had missed the night before.
100 pm I went to Burger King for lunch. Once I finished my lunch I got back to work on my homework for my Civil drafting design class.

The weekend
It has been a trying quarter that has been added to with the car problems that I am now going through. I have been working on homework for my classes that I have this week, but I am still looking for a car yet. I am hoping that I can find a car quickly. I would love to get that off of my mind and concentrate on finding a job and back on to my homework. I would love for things to get back to normal. I talked to my sister about planning a book release party for the book I had just released. Some of the days the work is different from other days, and I never know what challenge is going to come my way.

Chapter 8

OLSEN™

~ § ~

Many things have changed over the past year and a half, and the changes started with the death of my mother. Things moved fast after she had admitted to the hospital because she was having chest pains. My mom and my sisters Marilyn, Maxine and Anita helped me celebrated my birthday. My sisters and I went out to lunch together before I had to go get my physical at the VA medical center. One thing I had learned from my sister Marilyn that as she was holding me that I had did my duty on her.

She also told me that she remembered me as a baby wearing a blue ski suit. I've got a picture of me in that blue ski suit sleeping with a baby bottle at Fern Andersen's house. The early morning of the 29th of January my mom passed away from septic shock. Marilyn, Maxine and I were by her bed when she passed away. Donald started packing things up of mom's around the house once he had found that mom wasn't going to be coming home. The first thing I did I went to my oldest son's wrestling match and I had ran into the ex-wife and I told her that my mom had passed away and that I wanted to get together later to tell my son's, Lars and James that their Grand-ma had passed away earlier today. They were both more or less shocked with the news and really hadn't hit them yet that it was real.

I wasn't happy about that, and I told him I wasn't. I just sat around the house when I wasn't doing my studies and going to classes. Seating there looking at old family pictures become the one thing I did most of the day when I wasn't busy with school stuff. I would seat there thinking about family and how wonderful family was. Donald had run into the back of a semi with the pick-up. The pick-up was towed to a repair facility in Ontario, OR to be repaired. I had class that night but I couldn't leave the hospital. I texted my instructor and informed her that I wouldn't make it to class that night. I also informed my instructor what was going on and why I couldn't be in class that night.

My son Lars had a wrestling match in New Plymouth. I went to the match and saw the ex-wife there and explained to her that mom had passed away and I told her I needed to explain it to the boys that their Grandmother had passed away. I explained it to them and they were stunned at the news. While there I also took the chance to show Lars some the wrestling moves I had learned in high school. Mom had made some of the arrangements for her burial, but it was up to us kids to plan her funeral.

All of the kids and her granddaughter that live in New Plymouth and visiting daughter from Lake Charles met up at Schafer-Jensen Memorial chapel to discuss the arrangements for are mother's funeral. The family met with the funeral home operator to make arrangements and go through how and who would be participating in the funeral. Now that the arrangements were in place for the viewing and the funeral and the family had to wait for the day to arrive. While the pick-up was being repaired Donald had made arrangements with Gentry Ford to rent a car from them.

The day of the viewing had come for our mom. The family mulled around greeting the people who had come to the viewing. The ex-wife, Lars, James and her mom came to the view and they decided to stay and joined us at the dinner for the family at the Senior Citizen Center had prepared for the family.

They had come in while I was talking to Mrs. Brown and her daughter Tracy whom I hadn't talked to in a very long time. We didn't even get out of the funeral homes parking and Donald ran into the pole with the rental car wrecking it. Donald got mad at me because I didn't stop to check on him, but I was also headed for the dinner. The cops also had come to make out a police report about the wreck while we were at the dinner. The funeral parlor moves the casket with mom's body in it to the church. Meanwhile, Donald pays a visit to the church and places a notebook and pen in the casket with mom's body.

All of the family meets up at the church even family I hadn't seen in a while comes to mom's funeral. Mom's sister Agnes flew in from Seattle to be at her sister's funeral. We were surprised to see her, but we were happy to see her there, because we weren't sure that she would make it for her sister's funeral. There was one other surprise, there was police stationed at the doors of the church. Come the find out the police were there to keep Donald away from the funeral because Pastor Phil was scared Donald might try to do something.

A video was played during her funeral from pictures that I had supplied to the person who put together the DVD. I sat next to my older sister from Lake Charles during the funeral. George's daughter Shelly got up to speak and she said she was her Grandmas oldest grandchild, and when she said that I turned and looked to my sister Marilyn. I had to hold back from laughing at what she had said because I knew she wasn't the oldest grandchild.

Rod Elson got up to speak as well and mentioned what wonderful memories he had of mom and his Grandma Andersen. Then Pastor Phil went on with the rest funeral and after the prayer the Paul bears gather the carries the casket to the Hurst. I ferried Maxine and Martina to graveside service. Once there I joined the rest of the paul bears, so that we could the casket to the site she was to be buried at. Pastor Phil proceeded over the graveside service. During the grave side service, we released balloons and watched them float away.

He ended the grave side service with a wonderful prayer. Once through I walked back to my car to take Maxine and Martina back to the church for a family dinner. I invited the ex-wife, my kids and her mom to join us at the dinner, but I sat with my sisters Marilyn, Maxine, my nieces Martina, Stephanie and her mom. We sat there and eat while we visited with each other. Some family you only get to see once in a while because of distance and things going on in our lives.

The family gathered together at the house and started to go through things. George finally got his paperwork done to geo appointed executor of mom's estate and I had finally gotten my real estate license. A month had passed since the funeral and now the bank was forcing us to sell mom's house because of the reverses mortgage she had taken out against the house. Things that were of any real value George and Carol took along with Shelly and Frank taking the bedroom set of moms. George had gotten control of her and then all of the sudden he drives up to the house in a brand new pick-up.

Donald got moms van the one that he had wrecked and the one that mom didn't want him to drive but in the ended up getting any way because the pick-up got reposed. The pickup was in moms name and once she had passed it became part of her estate. Since my mom's death many things have changed in my life. The estate really to me hasn't been settled and her estate has brought out the worst in some of the members of my family. You also find out who the greediest of persons are in the family.

I am once again out on my own. I had just started to get to know my mom again after I had been away in the service. One the most enjoyable things were to watch Boise State Bronco football with my mom. I got a kick out of her getting really excited she would get after the Boise State Bronco football team would score a touchdown. It became one of the most enjoyable things that we shared together. It was the one thing that I had gotten my mom interested in. I had bought a BSU football jersey that I wear a few times, and after she had passed away I thought about putting the jersey in the coffin with my mom.

I know she would have shared in my success in getting my real estate license and finally my associate of arts degree in business administration finance. She would have enjoyed my successes yet to come. I finished typing up my mom's manuscript that she had written out, and I found out something things that I didn't know. It also made me think about a few things and it also filled in a few of the blanks. It also helped me to understand what Marilyn had told me about what had happened to her and her brothers.

In conclusion

~ § ~

I first published my life story titled "Always Aware: The journey of my life" I took a suggestion from a friend for the title of the book, and that is how I came up with the title for that book. In this book, pedigree charts that lay out the members of my family for the readers of this book. Ancestors that came to the United States from Norway via Denmark on 12th of July 1870, and German ancestry that dates back before the American Revolution. The ancestors I have on both sides of my family because Ole Petter's two sons married Conrad sisters.

When I was born in January my older sister Marilyn and my older brother Larry named me. About a year later, they were taken away and I wouldn't see them again after a few years had passed. When I was little I did see my dad leave for work, and then I went back to watching television. Comics that lasted on a Saturday for several hours, such as Flintstones, Space Ghost, Banana Split, Vulture Squadron, and Aqua Man. I also watched the Monkees and the Beatles.

In Kindergarden, I did like to be around one of the teachers I had for the classes, but not always did I get to be in her group. I started in one classroom in the first grade but then traded classes when they offered it to the class. The bus driver split the group on the bus because the bus was too crowded for all its passengers. Sometimes we would put up a real Christmas tree and then sometimes it would be a fake Christmas tree. We would have ham or turkey for Christmas dinner, because mom wanted to alternate what we had for the holiday dinner. The Norwegian ancestors had ham for their Christmas dinner. The ham was dedicated to the Norse god Frøy along with a special Christmas beer that drank from a horn.

It took me a while to finally get out of high school after high school I went to college for a year and a semester. I got married before I went into the U.S. Navy. I spent twenty years in the Navy and I got to see lots of other places while I was in. I learned a lot while I was in as well. I went back to college, and after I got out of the military I went back to college at Treasure Valley Community College. I got my degree in business. I am continuing my college education at ITT-Tech where I am studying Computer Drafting and Design.

It has been a life of ups and downs, but I also have met those ups and downs head on. Even though my dad told me that I wouldn't amount to much, but I set out to prove him wrong. I got a divorce and all the relationships I have had since ended in disaster. I was forced to move back home after the military and the relationship ended. I have been bouncing around from job to job ever since I have been out of the military. The jobs all have been back breaking jobs, and offered no challenges. College has also given me a chance to start my own business.

Starting my own business has presented its own ups and downs. I did make money in the market, but I also lost that money. The down turn in the market gave me a big chance to make money in the stock market. I could have made more money, but I chose to get out to soon. It was just one step in how I imagined how my life would be if I was debt free. I started to purchase some land in El Paso, TX, but couldn't afford the land any more. Buying the family house I have thought about doing as well. I never give-up on something I want to accomplish such as getting my real estate license and my business degree. A real estate I have set aside to pursue an Associate of Science degree in Computer Drafting and Design. I made a bad choice and now it has cost me my transportation to get to ITT-Tech, and to be able to finish out my last quarter of college.

Using what I am learning in my Computer Drafting and Design class to design the house I would like to buy and the future houses I would like to purchase. Knowledge and learning leds to success. I am updating my life's story and wrote down what I have learned about finances in a second book I have published. I used what I had learned in my English classes at ITT-Tech to write and even edit the book before I had it published. I am also using those skills to continue writing other books that I would like to get published in the future.

I don't dwell on what went wrong and happened in my life over the years. I have learned and moved on from those experiences in my life. Some of those experiences have been good and bad, but they have all added to the learning and who I am today. In a lot of ways I am better today for the experiences good and bad that I have been through over the years.

SOURCES

~ § ~

Emigration via Denmark [Cited 24 July 2012], Online: home.sol.no/-holum/dkutvweb3.html

www.ingramcontent.com/pod-product-compliance
Lightning Source LLC
Chambersburg PA
CBHW071015120626
46546CB00003B/1102

* 9 781962 868389 *